Senior Moments

a *tilted* look
at our
golden years

Adrea Nairne-Barrera

CASEY & HARK
Las Vegas, Nevada

Casey & Hark, publishers
Las Vegas, Nevada

caseyandhark@gmail.com

ISBN: 979-8-218-41671-3

book and cover designed by Sarah Bennett
shbennettbookdesign.com

Dedication

Senior Moments is dedicated to all my long-time friends who are either leading or following me in my travels through the golden years. Sometimes our promises to each other have outlasted marriages and crazy life events but all the time we march on, some with grace and others flopping all over the place.

I love you and treasure our times together.
As they used to sing on *The Golden Girls,*
thank you for being my friend.

Contents

The Way We Are

Dogs Rule

A Little Romance

Adventures with Food

It's Holiday Time

This & That

On the Road

Preface

After a particularly difficult time at age 60, my life completely changed. I had to put on my big girl pants and start a new way of living.

I began writing some of my experiences and looking at the world as a senior with all its absurdities and humor. I had no idea how much fun it would be to ramble on about the surprises of life after 60. Now I am well into my 70's and there are endless sources of material that pop up every day.

Then in 2012 I was invited to do a monthly column in the *Vegas Voice* called "60's to 60" about life in the 60's and being in your 60's. That lead to "Senior Moments" and a national award from NAMPA, the North American Mature Publishers Association.

In the spirit of fun, I keep forging ahead. I'm very qualified to write about baby boomer bungling, attitude, old habits, and of course attempts to adjust to the new technology.

The little things get me every time. Cleaning my closet, reading a menu, grocery shopping, body changes and even dating all have little built-in gifts when you are officially a senior. If you don't have a sense of humor, you'll never make it.

Nothing here is in any particular order and probably won't inspire you to change your life, but maybe you'll smile and relate to my observations. I truly hope you enjoy this collection of celebrations, adventures and complaints as much as I enjoyed writing them.

That's just fine with me!

Adrea
2024

The Way We Are

It must be my sparkling personality

I looked in the mirror the other day and really studied my whole self. It was funny, upsetting, discouraging, encouraging, irritating, embarrassing and overall, a moment frozen in my head forever.

I am frantically trying to assess myself. What do I really look like to others? How do I sound? Do I even make sense? What about all the dumb things I did and said that will catch up to me?

Staring in the mirror, I asked a bunch of questions and unlike the fairy tales, the face in the mirror didn't answer. All the face did was look stressed and puffy.

I will never again be the sassy girl getting random compliments. No dog whistles at construction sites! If you were ever a city dweller, you'll remember how innocent that used to be. In fact, I was very disappointed if it *didn't* happen. Times have certainly changed. Now we run for our lives if anyone looks at us with more than a passing glance.

Yes, I admit to being worried about my looks and no matter how hard I tried, size 5 never happened and bad hair days were much too common. The idea that one is not measured by looks really isn't clear in your youth. It can stick in the back of your head for a lifetime no matter how much therapy you've had.

So what's the point of all this? Well, I tried a little experiment and gained a whole new perspective in an unexpected way.

One day I asked "What is your favorite thing about me?" After the dazed look faded from my friend, she answered with conviction that I was loyal through good and bad times. Funny, *I thought the same thing about her!*

Then I asked my nail tech, hairdresser, friends and a few co-workers the same thing. Each time they looked confused that such a question would even be asked. A few seconds later I would get a smile and an answer.

One said I always ask how they're doing before discussing anything else. Another liked my sense of humor. A few mentioned my resilience. A colleague had respect for my work ethic. And my favorite was how I move forward past hardship and never lose hope for the future.

Not one person mentioned my looks or age. Though it may sound like I'm advertising myself when I write this, my real message is we get lost in measuring our worth by ridiculous standards.

When your friends answer the question as mine did, your self-image is improved in ways you never imagined. I'm told you shouldn't look to others for validation but every now and then, it doesn't hurt. And ladies, if your headlights become parking lights, don't worry!

So it must be my sparkling personality. The most dreaded words a woman could hear used to be "She may not be a knockout but she has a great personality." Now to this old girl, they have become most welcome. I sure never saw that one coming!

Senior housekeeping

The other day I was cleaning and realized my housekeeping routines reflect my lifestyle as I get older.

When the mail comes, if I remembered to get it, I create a stack in the kitchen. On cleaning day I methodically distribute things to their assigned locations. Magazine placement is assigned to the coffee table, my bathroom or his bathroom. Bills go on the desk under a chart that reminds me I have to pay them. If I ever lose the chart, I'll go without electricity.

When I find something to take to the cleaners, repair shop, or returned to the store, I pile it on top of my purse. This way I will notice it. When I leave the house, I still have to get my purse to find the car keys so the pile method works well. It always makes a lovely little mess but I feel better.

I hate doing dishes. If someone wants to use a real dish in our house and then offers to help clean up, I let them. I've grown fond of paper plates and as long as there are dollar stores, washing dishes isn't much of a problem. Unloading the dishwasher still presents some challenges.

Dusting is the most relaxed of the housekeeping sports. You use a soft cloth and some feather thing you can fling around the room while dancing to 70's songs. Disco and dusting go nicely together. Every gymnastic dance step gets you into the nooks and crannies of bookshelves.

Vacuuming is dangerous. After back surgery I discovered this chore can hurt me. Not giving in to limitations, I now vacuum sideways. As long as I don't pull anything, I can move side to side using my arms. The vacuum falls over from time to time so it takes a little longer.

Laundry is payback for something I'm sure I did. The same sideways action applies. I load the machines in a single, sweeping motion to toss it in or flip it out. Since I can't pull up, I flip things around and look for clean landing spots. Then it goes on the guest room bed for folding where it may remain for undetermined periods of time. If I forgot to fold while it was still warm, I might have to do it all over again.

Dog toys and other decorator items belong in the living room. Just ask our Golden Retriever. Every night after his dinner, our big dog carries his supper dish into the living room and places it by the couch. No one knows why. Every evening before dinner, he brings it back to the kitchen. The toys are scattered around to teach us to look where we're going.

My at-home glasses have a spot by the toaster oven. My going-out glasses stay in my purse. When they're moved, it takes my glasses to find my glasses presenting a whole new set of problems.

I've learned banker's boxes are furniture too and give you a place to put things at very little expense. I have grown attached to them. They eliminate the need to further sort papers by just marking them with the year. Whatever happened in 2012 is in a box. Easy and efficient.

Making the bed is an inconvenience for the smaller dog. He loves to perch on the highest part of the crumpled comforter. Thank you puppy!

I'm definitely in the golden age of housekeeping.

The shelf life of clothes

Our clothes say a lot about who we are. Some of us dress up every day, some more casual and others just grab the first thing they see in the closet whether the pieces match or not.

I prefer the casual approach so 90% of the time I'm wearing jeans. I may dress up with a really great top and, because I am a purse hoarder, I always carry something trendy or classic. Jewelry is limited to my wedding set and watch with an occasional light bracelet. Shoes are whatever is comfortable and heels are a thing of the past.

Today I can look into my closet and see more timeless outfits from days gone by. I have business suits, pants, skirts, dresses and blazers in perfect condition that have not been worn in years.

My body temperature is warmer these days so the 100% wool is useless even in the middle of winter. Higher body temperature is a little gift that comes with maturity.

The dresses were once worn with heels or boots. Maybe the boots thing will work around the holidays so I'll keep a few of those.

As for the blazers, they go great with the jeans and not with the body temperature. This is unwelcome conflict!

Now I have to make decisions. Our closet is too small and we can't move to satisfy space needs for clothes we don't wear. I actually thought about it and then realized I am downsizing now as fixed income takes over. Another gift received with maturity.

New in this equation is the actual "shelf life" of the clothes themselves. Where I used to wear my heart on my sleeve, once an endearing quality, I now wear odd things on my "shelf" from time to time. It isn't voluntary and has to be pointed out by well-meaning friends. And we're back to those endless gifts of maturity.

Nevertheless, this is a problem so I consider the cost of replacement in case of barbecue sauce or something else that won't come out. By the way, those little hints in the magazine only work in theory for most stains. Don't believe everything that has a seal of approval on it.

The biggest clothing changes are the crazy outfits I wear while in the house. Remember how we dressed up and Jack Jones sang about wives and lovers? And my all-time favorite line had to be "Put on your make-up." Sure.

We've come a long way baby! The hair is in a ponytail, make-up rarely on, if ever, little tennis socks are slippers and the garments required to hold this girl together are discarded the minute I get home.

Give me baggy t-shirts, stretchy shorts and elastic waists. The name of the game is comfort now. So to wrap this all up, I have to keep all the old stuff because they're baggy, stretchy and comfortable even when they have a few holes.

My closet is still stuffed. I tried.

The supermarket is not a vacation spot

Somewhere in the education system, students are learning that we, the consumers, are going to the supermarket to have a relaxing day strolling the aisles. Merchandising and marketing graduates march wide-eyed and eager into big city corporate offices completely disconnected from the areas they serve.

Some 30-year-old junior executive is making decisions on how we shop by looking at a computer screen and has never actually conversed with a shopper. We are reduced to zip code demographics. These fools are deciding what we like and what we don't like. The days of your friendly, neighborhood general store are long gone.

I once took a retail job in a moment of insanity thinking it might be fun a few years ago. I observed what attracted consumers to my window and displays. If I put something shiny and sparkly in the front of the store, the busloads of tourists came flocking in to look around. If I left it perfectly tailored and plain, color-coordinated and orderly, they passed by.

We became the highest grossing location in the west so they sent out a company merchandiser to ruin it.

A young lady arrives dressed in a business suit complete with attitude and a fake smile. Her patronizing comments were almost offensive as she explained that research shows we must dress the store back to the way it was before I took over. She spent 3 days merchandising, left town and within one month our numbers dropped to last place.

Then I resigned and politely explained I had another calling.

Now I'm a senior doing my grocery shopping and the store keeps changing. Do they have any idea how long it takes me to learn where everything is? I have my favorite market because I know my way around, not because of their prices.

Every time they do a modification to enhance my shopping experience, it takes me another 30 minutes to find what I need. If you want lettuce, you have about 4 places to find it depending on whether it's organic, packaged and chopped, house brand or loose. That's a lot of looking around for a salad.

How about yogurt and paper goods? You would think one would be in the dairy aisle and the other in the paper goods section. Nope, not even close. Yogurt has 3 places depending on brand. Paper towels are with detergents and toilet paper is with baby products. Who came up with that?

When you get to the checkout, the cashier asks you to donate to something and then asks if you know about their special programs. And yes, I know about your stupid programs and I'm not spending another hour on the computer checking things off and then more time trying to find it in the store!

You moved it anyway so what's the point?

With Thanksgiving this month, I plan to devote a minimum of 2 hours to find what I need for dinner. Last year it only took me 20 minutes.

Going to the market is a chore we have to do. Make it easy for me and I'll go more often. Make it harder and I'll go out to eat.

We now go out a lot.

I just paid my bills! OMG!

I now know the true meaning and proper time to say "OMG!" I listen to others say it, TV shows use it in titles and everyone texts and emails that same tag on anything requiring an exclamation. English teachers and grammarians are helpless to do anything about it.

But once in a while, a trend that seems utterly stupid at first becomes a cliché because it works. When I finished paying my bills this month, "OMG" was entirely appropriate.

It started very routinely reviewing all the utility statements, health care and housing costs. Such are the usual ongoing expenses of daily life.

With Medicare now in the picture, I was, for the first time, glad to have reached 65. That in itself was a bit different than I expected. No one ever used to look forward to being older so it definitely deserves an "OMG!"

We wait for movies to come on cable so we can relax at home for movie night. Cable offers endless streams of things you would never actually go out to see. So what's a little $5.99 movie every now and then? Don't ask.

My grocery bill went up. At first, nothing looked different until I remembered you're getting less in the same box at the price you paid for more. It took a while for me to notice but I've got it now.

Our car insurance went up. We now drive less and are semi-retired so how did that happen? We have multi-car, multi-line, accident-free and every discount imaginable but there you have it! It went up.

Our dogs are our kids and get whatever they need. As they age, they need doggy drugs and things. There is no insurance unless you thought of it when they were 8 weeks old. If so, you would have paid premiums over 10–15 years instead of $300.00 per month now.

I'm pretty sure we're ahead on that one. Anyway, they're like children that never grow up and get their own place and that's fine.

So next I ventured out to see what I could do in bulk and prorate the cost over 3 months. The OMG's just kept coming!

Ultimately I determined buying 72 rolls of bulk toilet paper was no cheaper than grabbing 12-packs on sale at the grocery store. At our age we can't buy gallons or 5-pound sacks of anything because it will spoil before we eat it.

I suppose if I knew how to can things, I would make use of all that bulk. Then I would have to give it away which defeats the whole purpose.

Frozen bulk packs are good if you don't mind the added cost of a 2nd refrigerator running in the garage in 110 degree heat. (*My husband's pet peeve.*)

I have a list of which stores will save me more on daily use items. Getting to them ate the difference so I pitched the list.

I also don't go 20 miles to a specific gas station to save 80 cents when I can just as easily roll my car down the hill and save 20 cents and 2 hours.

The only way to save is to live in a group home. OMG!

Girl stuff never really changes

There's probably a study somewhere on what girls do and talk about at various stages of their lives and since I'm a girl, I think I'm qualified to say, it never really changes from 16 to 66.

As teenagers, there were boys, make-up, clothes, tanning, curfews, private phone lines, wedding dresses, movie stars, bras, television shows, and anything promising to make us look more grown up.

As seniors we have a different perspective but the subjects never change. The main topic is still men and everything that follows seems to circle around that bliss we call coupling or independence, depending on what we prefer.

Boys to men starts with endless phone calls announcing to the world that he looked at me and smiled! Now when he looks at me, I wonder what he's going to ask me to do.

Make-up then had Cleopatra eyes, false eyelashes, heavy foundation and the teased hair. Sometimes I even put a bow in my hair. Really? The bow isn't an option these days. (*Remember Rose Marie on the* Dick Van Dyke *show?*)

In my early 20's, I did the beach thing and had a tan for 5 years. Sunscreen was reserved for my eyelids, nose and lips only. The rest of me was slathered in moisturizers and oils. How I escaped skin problems still amazes me and I'm grateful. Now I have absolutely no brightness to me at all.

Curfews were an arguing point with my parents. Now I am looking for any reason to go home early so I don't fall asleep at someone's house after dinner. Did my parents gave me a curfew so they could go to bed too?

We've progressed from private phone lines as the ultimate teenage status gift to email. And only a few dream of wearing Mom's pin-tucked wedding gown handed down from her Mom anymore. Now they get married on the beach in flip-flops. Personally I think the beach is much more fun and costs less until they pick Hawaii, Italy or Jamaica at a 5-star resort.

So when the girls get together, we still have the same agenda, only updated to the "now."

The girl talk is about cover-ups for age spots and wrinkles, finding stretchy clothes that are fashionable and not see-through, discussing the SPF number which has reached an all-time high of 50 nowadays, getting home before we fall asleep, movie stars that still manage to look OK versus those that look like dolphins from too many face lifts, lingerie to flop down on the couch and watch TV, and just about anything to make us look *less* grown up.

But once in a while that old spark gets us and we look at our partners and feel young again, remembering the day we first felt those butterflies. So the pretty stuff comes out of the closet, the make-up goes on, we flirt and set up a romantic evening and all is right with the world.

Ain't love grand? Have a great Valentine's Day and make a new story to tell the girls!

If nothing is wrong, we have nothing to talk about

I have a handful of long-time dear friends that I speak to on a regular basis. Some are more regular than others. Weekly, monthly or longer, we still can pick up conversations and keep up with each other. And, of course, it's the girl talk continuation.

So as life moves along over these last 40 years, there are marriages, kids, divorces, loss, money problems, illness and adventure that take up most of the conversations. But have you ever noticed when everything is going just great, the conversations don't take very long?

As a follow-up to Girl Stuff Never Really Changes, there is an element that I neglected to mention:

If no one is divorcing or broke, you're stuck. No complaining about high prices or the ever-so-popular "he's a jerk" or "she's a bitch" commentary. Discussing doctor visits is a time consumer but if no one is going to the doctor, you can't ask "What's wrong?"

The vacation story after all these years can actually be boring. Whoopee for you on your *faaaabulous* vacation that I didn't get to experience because I was stuck here in 110 degree heat!

And the grandchildren? Please, by all means, take out 200 photos of kids I don't know and let me exclaim their cuteness holding a Barbie doll. Now if there's a puppy involved, I might like that.

As for the house, I agree it's time to get a single story because the stairs are harder and harder to climb. But no, I can't help you move because my back is no better than yours.

Am I crabby? I don't think so at all. I just find it very funny that if nothing is wrong, our calls are shorter. We don't use up time being happy for each other but instead use up time only when showing sympathy and understanding for unfortunate events. I can make an "ooooh and aaaah" and "so sorry to hear that" last for hours.

Everyone agrees we have more to be watchful about as we age, however studies also show we get too wrapped up in drama and the old self-fulfilling prophecy takes over. If you focus too much on it, it will eventually go wrong leading to longer conversations.

For those who thrive on lengthy, draining exchanges, this is good news indeed!

My solution is simple. Keep a list of daily victories and share them weekly with your friends. Make them listen and then you'll be giving them tons of reasons to complain to their friends how boring *their* lives are or how boring it is listening to you.

Either way, it's a win-win for everyone. You can provide entertainment for all. Sometimes you have to effect attitude adjustment in stealth mode.

See yourself as an inspiration to others and walk away leaving a little positive energy behind. It's really not as twisted as it sounds.

Every time you share positive thoughts, you make your life better and a lot more fun. There's nothing wrong with putting a little mischief into the mix once in a while. You might make the crabbiest and most drama-obsessed person you know start thinking about what's right instead of what's wrong.

Embrace your batwings!

Yippee! **It's a new year!** Many of us spent December eating our way through holiday events with food involved.

First we were swamped with advice on what to eat, how to cook, portion size and not being rude to our hosts. Then, somewhere in the middle of the month, we saw new ads for diet centers and exercise memberships from experts ready to take over our care following a month of total indulgence.

These experts really believe we're going to make diet resolutions on January 1st and achieve lifestyle change by following their system. Probably not. If the permanent change actually worked, they would all be out of business. Anyone ever think about that?

About 20 years ago I thought magic diet supplements, new food programs and a personal trainer held the keys to success. I looked forward to moments of great cuteness once again. I had a few however they became further and further apart.

The decade of my 40's was my favorite because I was old enough to know what I wanted and young enough to do it. So I ate stuff, did stuff and all-around stayed active and a little spoiled. Since I've never been perfect anyway, a few pounds here and there were easy to manipulate.

Imagine my surprise when I learned about blood sugar and other little things like trans fats, LDL to HDL, portion control, carbs and the ever-so-lovely balanced approach to good health. That sure messed me up. Now I worry about what is sprayed on stuff, why I have air bubbles when I eat the proper foods and each time I feel something tingle, I'm sure it's a new disease.

For all the ladies who have batwings and folds in new places, and gentlemen who don't even drink and have beer bellies, welcome to the party! Find a seat because it gets crowded around here.

January is when we take inventory. How much do we weigh? How much should we eat? How much do we really need to eat? And the ultimate how can we sneak in the fun stuff and still do the moderation thing?

I had a great excuse for not moving the earth to get to my ideal weight. My so-called ideal weight was always at least 25 pounds away, so I held with the notion that losing would make me look like a Shar-Pei puppy. I absolutely love all dogs but I didn't see myself wearing a collar and leash, even under the best circumstances.

Now I have no choice. I have to do this diet thing to get a good report card at the doctor every few months. I feel like I'm in school again studying for blood test exams. If my numbers are good, I get to have something really gooey and decadent. If not, back to packaged food and doom.

Valentines Day is next month and that means chocolate! Maybe if I eat enough veggies and fat-free salad dressing, I can have a treat?

In the meantime, I tell you all, embrace your batwings and other disturbing body parts. Stay healthy and don't stress if you droop a little more than before. I celebrate that I got this far in the first place. That's good enough for me.

My signature thing

Most of the women I know have a signature "thing" they either collect, say or wear. Friends with the same interest trade back and forth and I'm no exception.

Mine is purses. Having spent so much time in California, I quickly got absorbed in the label status game during my 20's which, thank God, I got over in later years.

Not lost to me however was the aspect of high quality versus a sale at the swap meet. That swap meet Gucci fell apart in a month but the real one lasted so long that I kept looking for ways to damage it.

It is nearly impossible to destroy a Fendi, YSL, Chanel, "Louie," Cartier, Martini or just about any true designer bag from 25 years ago. Spend $1000 back then and your purses cost $40 a year when you pencil it out.

The problem with quality is it lives up to its name. I have old designer purses that have fallen into the ocean, been run over by the car, had iced tea spilled inside and countless other mishaps and they still look just fine.

Except for a little wear and tear on the leather bindings, no one would ever know. And, you can contact the manufacturer so they can replace straps and bindings at minimal cost! Whoa!

I still have vintage Dooney & Bourke when they made all-weather leather and actually lined it in leather too. The bag weighs a ton but it looks really sharp.

Now I go into the closet and see the same old, same old. I am so bored but I have no excuse to shop because there's nothing wrong with what I have. That goes back to mother's sensibilities.

Last summer I got a new purse when I traded with my oldest, dearest friend who has the same fever I do. Now think I won the lottery. With prices so high, I would never buy another one new when they now cost as much as 1 or 2 house payments. Not cool.

In a moment of insanity, I once looked at a designer pet carrier and realized the cost of that could save 100 rescue dogs. I think that was my sobering wake-up call.

Now I just put the little dog in a tote bag from Target and off we go. He's perfectly happy and doesn't know the difference.

I'm not saying I'm ever going to be completely over the designer purse "thing" however I have new rewards like the watch giveaway at the M worth about $1. It's a great blue-turquoise color made of rubber, keeps great time and makes your wrist sweat after 5 minutes.

And then there are pillow color changes in the house so everything will look updated. That's a whole lot of time in Home Goods, Pier One and Kirklands. I'm keeping busy for now.

So my purse collection stays in rotation......except when Coach gives you 50% off everything in the store, even the clearance, and you get that feeling you've struck gold. Control takes a hike.

So who wants to talk about shoes?

She's broad where a broad should be broad

Lately I find myself listening to a 50's or 60's station on the car radio and of course I know almost all the words to almost all the songs. I can't remember what's on my grocery list but I can strut through the store singing "tan shoes and pink shoelaces."

And I can also remember what I may have been feeling when they were first played. Strange as it may seem, those impressions never fade.

Now we live in a world that criticizes everything and even goes so far as to criticize old standards like "Baby It's Cold Outside" as being sexist. Some even have banned it from elevator playlists.

Has anyone seen *South Pacific* lately? It was just on TCM and I watched on a lazy Sunday afternoon. Mitzi Gaynor sings that "she's broad where a broad should be broad." The song is about Honeybun who is 101 pounds of fun filled with dynamite. That makes her a plaything, right? *Horrors!*

In the storyline, she runs from the man she loves because he had been married to a Polynesian woman so his children were mixed. We have discrimination and more sexism all in a sure fire hit! How about a demonstration on Broadway?

One of my all-time favorites is the Jack Jones hit song "Wives and Lovers." It was a running joke between me and my late husband. He would tease me about no make-up, jeans and a ponytail instead of make-up, fancy hair and dresses. If that song were released today, women would be marching in protest. You don't hear it on the radio much anymore.

When the Duprees sang "You Belong To Me" I was young and dreamed of the day when I would be the subject of a song like that. Now we're offended if we belong to anyone. We're not possessions last I heard.

Moving on, 2019 and rap has hit an all-time high along with the resurgence of loud banging and no melody. If you can even understand the rap, your body can't dance to it anymore. I give it a three.

If you do understand it, sorting out the violence from the good message is another impossible task. It's also hard to hear anything when they're just banging around in the percussion section.

Over and over I keep saying I grew up in a time where a little whistle or a role model like June Cleaver was not a bad thing. It was reflected in our music and TV even though couples couldn't sleep in the same bed.

I continue to sing along with my oldies and just make sure no millennials are around.

I'm still adopted

This month's subject may be controversial for some, but for me it is part of my life's journey and may strike a chord for anyone who has been on either side of this equation. I'm adopted and have been part of many adult searches over the years, including my own.

The search, challenges and wonder of being adopted is a subject that raises questions about responsibility and the right to know one's background.

In the early days of adoption search, we used medical history to justify our actions. Social acceptance for adoptees, birth parents and adoptive families was never guaranteed. Much was discussed behind closed doors. We would like to think progress has been made over these last 6 decades, but sadly it has not been enough.

Part of an article I wrote many years ago read "Adoption was never a problem for me. It seemed only to affect the strangers around me. Growing up I repeatedly made a conscious effort to overlook feelings of alienation put upon me by others. What an unfair burden to ask a child to carry."

My family protected me from neighbors who were shocked when I would openly say I was adopted. It was the 1950's and one didn't speak of such things. My parents always jumped in and made certain there was no shame in my honesty. As an adult, I'm eternally grateful to them for keeping my place in the family normal.

My search for my birth mother in 1983 had a good conclusion. She passed away a few years later but knowing me and that I had been raised by loving parents was an answer to silent prayers. Things were finally resolved.

Today I have yet to complete the search for my birth father. Though I believe he is no longer alive, the history of my creation still has importance to me.

What is really still at issue is the basic rule of one's right to know. As children, we are the subject of a contract made by adults supposedly in our best interests. As children, that makes sense.

Whatever social stigma is felt by the birth parents doesn't eliminate the responsibility for having given birth to a child. I exist because someone gave birth to me. That's not going away.

Unfortunately the contract of secrecy made for me does not expire when I am an adult. No matter how old I am, I will never be released from that document. I do not have equal rights under the law to obtain my own birth information. That's just plain wrong.

I have no false expectations about great reunions. That boat sailed many moons ago. The ancestry craze of today still excludes me. Adoptees and birth parents are still in a world of discrimination by laws that have long outlived their purpose.

The right to know should be given once the minor reaches adulthood. I really hope I live to see everyone have the choice of what they want to know and what they don't. In the meantime, I'm still adopted and subject to different rules.

If someone in your family is searching, I hope you'll support them no matter where the path leads.

My body is a garden

My body is a garden of weeds and flowers. It sprouts things, sheds stuff and all around assures me every day I am still growing and fully fertilized.

Women go from tweezing eyebrows to tweezing chins. Shaving legs has expanded to a few unmentionable places. Hair that once withstood perms, hair color and curling irons, now sheds in the shower.

Texture and moisture balance has changed too. Skin treated with lotion every day for decades now has little areas drooping at the inner elbow when you hold your arms out. Unless your arm is fully extended, you can't hide it.

And the grey hair, now colored, has a texture that resists styling. There are wiry little ends sticking out around my face.

And how about those other hairs? Good grief! You would think as we get older, nature would give us a break. Who made that decision? Men's ears, noses, women's chins, cheeks?

We survived acne as teens, stress wrinkles, bought thousands of creams and now earned our place in the golden years. We deserve clear skin, pretty hair in the right places, and bodies that shouldn't require so much maintenance.

I have also figured out why the older we get, the shorter we cut our hair. It's about the heat generated on the back of the neck and nothing else. The style is secondary.

Skin moisture balance is a biggie for the beauty companies. I am slightly offended when the advertisers target a woman of 40 to sell the latest creams. There's nothing wrong with anyone at 40 and many live with their baby boomer parents. Aren't they targeting the wrong consumer?

All this talk of "60 is the new 50" and "50 is the new 30" can really mess you up. It would stand to reason that 40 would then be the new 20 and personally, I don't think I would even want to be 20 again. I certainly wouldn't need age-defying treatments either.

I'm not crazy about these changes happening to me. In reality it's been happening for a long time but each little surprise lead me to another way of disguising it. Not so simple now!

I've always said one should embrace change, and batwings. These days the list includes more stuff requiring gardening skills and you need strong glasses to do it.

For at least one day a week, I park myself on the couch and watch some old TV show from the 70's or 80's and imagine hanging around with those guys as I was then. No chin hairs, strong, natural nails we wrapped in tea bag paper (remember Juliette nails?) and I make popcorn.

To my readers old and young, please don't misunderstand. I am pretty happy with who I am. I only wish it didn't require as much work to control these little inconveniences.

When my husband looks at me and suggests I may want to check out something in the mirror, it isn't criticism. I thank him because I can't see the damn thing and everyone else can.

The UPS guy should be delivering the 10X magnifying mirror any day now.

Ahhhhhh, the golden years!

Don't worry, it's just a cold

Now I'm on the back side of my 60's and in pretty decent shape except for the usual denial that I've slowed down. So when I get sick, I really don't expect it to disrupt my life.

Back when I was a kid, if I got a cold, my mother filled a bowl with hot water and made me put a towel over my head and breathe in the steam. I remember sitting in the bathroom with the bowl on the hamper waiting to feel better. Like magic, it always worked!

If I had a fever, our doctor would come over, check me out and give us whatever was needed for me to get better.

Fast forward to 2015, catch a cold and you're hopelessly lost in a maze of regulations where no doctors come to see you unless you shell out hundreds of dollars for a house call. And pharmacies don't deliver on some medications.

I got a cold and tried my very best to tough it out. After 2 weeks of "No I'm not sick" and "Yes I am sick," it went from an occasional sneeze to all out misery. Everything hurt. I had that awful cough with no relief and Friday was just a day away. I found about 3 tablespoons of old cough medicine from 2011 still in the cabinet so clearly that wouldn't make it through the weekend.

Add to the mix all the aches and inconveniences of hacking, rib pain and sinuses ready to explode at any moment. Then each cough leads to the probable need for diapers. To those who have ever experienced it, no further explanation is required.

So I dragged myself to my doctor who prescribed antibiotics (now I had a fever too) and a new bottle of cough syrup. Then I dragged myself to the pharmacy but they were out of the cough syrup so I had to go to another one.

The 2nd pharmacy said my Medicare doesn't cover it because they don't want to be responsible for me falling down because the cough syrup could make me dizzy. Really?

Let me get this straight. Medicare will pay for narcotic pain killers but I need 4 ounces of cough syrup so my cough doesn't blow my head apart and they're worried about me falling? That cost me $47.00 and I had to sign disclosures.

By the time this goes to press, I hope to be over all this. Right now I'm still making horrible noises when I sleep and I cough for no reason at all. It seems the older I get, the longer things take to get out of my system.

I would much prefer that good stuff lingered instead of coughs and sniffles. We should be on a reward system for surviving embarrassing moments and outbursts of sneezes, gunkies and yelps.

When you're sick with something considered a discomfort and hardly a reason to stay home, you expect it to be done in a couple of days. It takes longer than recovering from surgery! But don't worry, it's just a cold.

The worst client ever!

They say a doctor makes the worst patient and a lawyer makes the worst client so since my profession wasn't included in those all-too-familiar sayings, I never figured it applied to me. Now, after over 20 years in real estate, I become my own client when we decided to buy a new house. The experience was awful!

It is daunting to watch every step of the process with expert eyes and knowledge that one teeny weeny, minuscule, insignificant piece of information can set the whole transaction toppling over. Where were you 5 years, 26 days and 2 hours ago?

Each letter of explanation about things no longer in my short term mind file must be memorialized. Just answer the question. Don't answer more than you are asked. Account for gaps even if it was because you had the flu.

Explain every deposit, including the check your sister sent to buy her something she saw in Las Vegas last time she visited. And not to mention we kept my late husband's car for my grandson but it was garaged in California so explain that too.

I've always been aware and considerate of my client's needs to know. How each step of the process impacts them is part of the job so when a stupid thing comes up, I typically resolve it myself or present it in a manner designed to limit anxiety. I've gotten pretty good at it too.

Here I was, dreading each email from the loan processor as we assemble documents. My husband was working out of state while this went on. He signed everything and trusted that I would never put us into anything less than perfect. No pressure!

So I missed the part where the closet door collides with the bedroom door. And when the vent over the microwave came flying off when turned on, I was a bit surprised. The house passed all inspections on major operating systems but I was a typical buyer looking at how pretty it was and not paying attention. As an agent, I would have caught all that stuff.

I can't remember how many conversations I've had over the years preparing clients for the business and drama of real estate.

"Be ready to hate the process" or "Don't go overboard or buy anything new until we close" and so on, and so on. And inevitably someone will say or do something that threatens everyone's peace of mind so call your real estate agent and let a professional handle it. Huh?

I wish I had someone like me to shield me from the ups and downs but it's like going to see a movie with a special effects pro. Years ago I went to see *ET* with a film person who spent the entire movie criticizing the little alien and his movements. TMI my friends!

I deal with really complicated transactions, bank negotiations, 1st timers and all the way to the other extreme of investors and owners making changes.

Some are simple and some not so much but they all have one thing in common: They deserve service and resolution coupled with the voice of reason. I never ruin the experience the way my friend ruined *ET* for me.

I really do know my name

When you have name like mine, everyone wants to correct it. I have even had a computer auto-correct a document for me. There are some things technology should just leave alone!

The origin of my name and its spelling came from my parents, Adolph and Regina. They liked the name Adrea because it used letters from both their names. There is another spelling with the "i" but very few "Adrea" people running around.

I seldom get confused with Adrienne but the Andrea name haunts me always. It seems people have a duty to correct it to the acceptable version in their view.

But when it comes to acceptable names, in the world of celebrity kids names such as "Moon," "Apple," and "North," what does any of it matter anymore? At least the computer accepts the spelling but the names are kind of ridiculous.

I have an email that uses my name in the address and I think there's an Andrea out there getting a lot of things she doesn't understand. I hope she finds them interesting.

Many years ago, in another lifetime, I was at a formal university dinner and the Dean spent time before the event learning everyone's name for introductions. As you might guess, when he introduced my husband, he added "and his lovely wife Audroonia."

I even tried to get the domain name adrea.com but it's taken by some foreign entity involved in a lawsuit last time I checked. Been working on that one for about 10 years.

Then I re-married and my name changed to Adrea Nairne. That quickly became "Adrean Airne" or "Adrea Narne" or "Adrea Marine" and variations so convoluted that I can't remember them all.

And here I am some 60+ years into this with a hyphenate name Adrea Nairne-Barrera. Since I still work as Adrea Nairne, I haven't changed professionally but I'm sure there will be some very interesting versions soon enough.

The real problem happens once someone makes a wrong entry and it follows you forever. The computer has not allowed us to correct it.

Even if you catch the mistake quickly, information has instantly been sent to every conceivable entity connected to the original source. Retrieving and starting again cannot be done.

Let's look at passwords and identification. There are currently 3 sites that refuse to accept that I am Adrea. They have even sent alerts & denied me access as I try to do business on line. Since my email has the correct spelling, you would think there would be a recognition factor in there.

If I respond to the email with the correct spelling, doesn't it make sense to allow me the right name on the website?

The oddest part is that Adrea is a simple 5-letter combination. You don't need to speak another language nor is it derived from a longer version. It's just 5 letters people!

I would love to share stories with people whose names contain 10 to 25 letters. They must have plenty to share.

September 21, 1967

To most of us, Susan Oliver was the guest star of the 60's appearing in just about every show on television. She is remembered as the "green girl" of *Star Trek* fame and so many shows even the internet can't keep up with her credits.

To me, she was my friend for a while and a woman who left an impression that grows more and more significant as I get older. She was way ahead of her time, educated, beautiful and genuine.

I met her in the late 70's and when I visited her home, I walked into a huge room with memorabilia scattered around as she was writing the book about her 1967 solo flight across the Atlantic.

Her property was nestled in the hills off Mulholland Drive with a main house and a guest house. It was quiet and welcoming.

Looking at her delicate beauty, one would never imagine the strong woman inside who, on September 21st, 1967, took off from La Guardia Airport in New York on a solo flight headed for Moscow. Fully prepared for the journey, she even spoke fluent Russian.

Susan piloted her own Aero Commander 200 and would be only the 2nd woman to fly solo across the Atlantic from New York City. Unfortunately the Soviet Union would not let her fly in Soviet air space so her flight ended in Denmark.

In 1983 her book was published and though she received numerous awards for aviation, including Pilot of the Year co-piloting a Piper Comanche and winning the 2,760 transcontinental 1970 Powder Puff Derby, her interests turned to directing in later years.

The 60's were turbulent to say the least and our memories of old shows and music now streamed through cable and the internet focus on a lot of trivia. If I hadn't known her, I never would have imagined her accomplishments.

So let's celebrate the amazing women whom we never imagined had the guts, intelligence and determination to break out with grace and dignity. Susan was one of those great women and we miss her spirit every day.

The last time I saw Susan was in the 80's when my life changed and we lost touch. It broke my heart to hear she was losing her battle with cancer and passed in 1990. Much too young and had she gone on, I know she would have thought up something new and exciting to do.

The next time you see her on nostalgia television, think of her flying alone over the Atlantic at a time in our history when women were just breaking the stereotype. We loved her then but I think I love her more now.

Compliment, insult or harassment?

In July, 2013 I wrote about how one goes from the age of compliments and dog whistles at construction sites to maturity. How we measure ourselves now is very different.

Growing up in the city, a whistle was a good barometer and harmless. Our role models were Sophia Loren, Marilyn Monroe and sexy, sexy, sexy.

Fast forward and things have gotten completely out of control. It's pretty overwhelming.

I too was a victim of sexual harassment in the mid 70's on the job. My employment was threatened but I didn't give in. The incident was noticed by the president of the company and he apologized and said I wouldn't be fired.

Looking back, why would I be fired? I didn't do anything. I didn't bother to see if I had recourse and life went on. No one told us there were rules.

Where do we draw the line? And when a woman takes money to keep quiet, she is in fact responsible for using the incident to gain something. Coming back later doesn't work for me unless she gives back the money. She sold herself out.

But, in her defense, options were limited and the support was not there. So at what point would a woman of the 60's and 70's have been given credibility when the power was on the other side?

I am not including serial offenders and predators but I do have concerns that pretty soon no man will be able to compliment a woman in the workplace without the risk of being reported. And not all women are innocent either!

Accountability has to go both ways. I made my choice in the 70's and in 2018, I can't go back and change that decision. Now we have different guidelines for the behaviors when years ago we accepted "boys being boys" and no one did anything unless there was physical & sexual abuse involved.

Does that make it right then and wrong now? Again, of course not but how we measured offensiveness was different. We wore mini-skirts and "come & get me" boots so if a man wanted to make an advance, he might go to that little dog whistle moment even at work. And we smiled.

Women have come a long way in 40 years and this will take some time to sort out. I commend those standing and making their voices heard. I also condemn the ones who see it as an opportunity to have 15 minutes of fame by lying.

I have great respect for those who endured mistreatment and lost opportunities. Perhaps our children and grandchildren will also learn to respect each other no matter what sex they are.

To bag or not to bag

Contrary to what anyone might think, this is not about grocery bags, the environment or even designer handbags. This is about the gifts some of us get as we age known as eye bags, affectionately referred to in my world as face pillows.

They sneak up very quietly and then one day someone takes your picture and there are these little half-moons under your eyes. At first I blamed it on the lighting.

No amount of concealer covers it up or removes the shadows of eye bags. Suntans don't help because bags don't tan. Anyway we now know we have to stay out of the sun and the paler you are, the more fashionable you are. That too is not an attractive alternative.

So now I am stuck with these damn things and my research begins on what to do about it. The choices are interesting.

The whole cucumber routine just looks exotic on a spa website but in reality, slapping cold cucumbers on your eyes for 25 minutes seems just silly.

You can also slice raw potatoes and wear them or grate & squeeze the juice to apply under your eyes.

Did you know you can put honey under your eyes when you go to bed too? How long would it take the dogs to start licking it off?

There's also almond oil, cold used tea bags and a mix of buttermilk and turmeric, all recommended as natural treatments for eye puffiness.

As for the beauty treatments with time lapse photos advertised on TV, they actually create a film to tighten the area and when you wear make-up, it peels off anyway or looks funny.

A few hints popped up on allergy control, no salt and sleeping on your back to avoid pooling fluid in the eye area. If I sleep on my back, the snoring that follows is not appreciated.

Many years ago before magic potions that cost $200 for ¼ ounce, there was Preparation H. I heard that solution long before I knew what hemorrhoids or eye bags were. I just can't make the connection.

The usual catch-all is following a diet rich in iron, veggies, fruit, potassium, and be happy. Crying is a no-no for obvious reasons.

The most drastic of course is surgery that sucks the pillow out. You'll have black eyes for a while but when you heal, you'll look great. Or so they say.

My solution is simple. I smudge the bags out of every photo. I leave just enough shadow to be genuine and I never retouch my wrinkles because I earned every single one of them.

Once again, I complain and do nothing.

I'm too old for my car

All my life I have resisted reading directions. I can remember my mother giving me a new toy and showing me what it did only to have me state firmly that I could do it myself. Instructions took the fun out of the puzzle.

Brat that I may have been, I usually figured it out and would show her my great accomplishment. Thank goodness she had a sense of humor and appreciated my independence. However I now face the ultimate test.

Here I am, 60 years later, taking on the challenges of a new car. It may be silly but my old car and I were dear friends. When she threw her 3rd drive prop, it was time for retirement.

I loved that car and understood every squeak, click, hum and burp she made. She didn't have a backup camera or Bluetooth and ate gas. Even the needle nose pliers needed to release the parking brake, the cane to hold up the tailgate and the floppy visors didn't shake my confidence.

Along comes my defining moment of choice and I picked a crossover SUV for warranty, economy and safety. All very good reasons to be happy but I'm out of my element. Nothing is familiar.

There are no shades coming up from the doors, the side mirrors don't flex if I'm too close to the ATM, the windows don't automatically rise with a tap and I am lower to the ground now. This is all in the name of smart choices. And there's a payment! OMG I am freaking out since it's been years since I've had one.

And to add insult to injury, I picked a vehicle with great ratings but as we age, insurance companies raise your rate with your age even if you have a perfect driving record. What was the point of being perfect?

Let's talk about electronics in these new modes of travel. I did not buy the top model. I stayed true to my plan of moderation and yet it has strange things going on.

It flashes when a car is in my blind spot, reads texts, shuts down at lights to save gas and scares the crap out of me, has backup cameras with lines in 3 colors, is key-less but the fob has a key anyway and no keyhole, fog lights that become turn lights, no rear opening window and a crash alert going off with no provocation near trees.

The instruction book is several hundred pages of diagrams and charts so I'll be busy for a while. By the time I finish understanding this, I'll be trading it in.

OK Mom! I'm reading directions!

I still need prep time

The amount of time it takes to double back, look to see if you've actually closed the garage door, check that you have your phone and your regular glasses, along with your sunglasses, makes rushing out the door pointless.

Yes I have gone out with different shoes on my feet. I change my purse to a smaller one hoping I can fit everything in and later find that it's like carrying a can of sardines so you can't get anything out until it ALL falls out.

I keep hairbrushes and ponytail bands in the car just in case and then I wear them out of the car. Somewhere in Henderson there are about 200 ponytail bands hiding with all the missing socks from the dryer.

And let's talk about the pills. I have to take a couple of things daily so I pack them in a pillbox along with regular Tylenol, Advil and whatever allergy med I'm using that year. I am a walking drug store so my husband depends on me for such things. Re-loading it is another task I screw up and inevitably one of us needs what I don't have.

If I'm on my way to work, I have folders. Doesn't everyone have folders? You put them on the passenger seat but if they're facing the wrong way, braking for a light will toss them all out on the floor. And unless you stay with the sardine-packed purse, a tip of that produces very bad results.

Remembering my watch, ring and accessories before going out the door, making sure all the dogs have been out and grabbing lists takes time. I try really hard to keep things simple but the older I get, the more complicated it seems to be.

Calculating the right time to leave the house never goes well for me. While my husband is out the door tapping his foot, I'm still doing double checks. The dogs hate me for leaving and I spend the day questioning the garage door status. Overall, rushing is very tricky.

And I'm exhausted.

Dirty fashions

The other day I was in a nice restaurant waiting for an order when I noticed how everyone was dressed. When you're sitting in a bar area, you see all.

Nobody looks fresh! There is no such thing anymore and I am longing for the fashion police to turn the tables on us and make men shave, get the crap out of their hair, and look like men again.

As for the women, I guess they save money because those old, torn jeans are the rage. Attach some rhinestones, add a little lace and you're today's fashion statement. Just look at the ads in Town & Country to see tattered jeans with a $3,000 handbag. I think it also has something to do with where the rips and tears are to determine if the jeans are old or cost another $800.

Tattoos, once reserved for bad boys are a badge of honor for some. The more you have, the more your status goes up. Women are on the list too. I understand a permanent mark to remember something or someone, a lost love, a cause or symbol of your faith. I don't understand skulls and all the weapons art burned into someone's skin forever.

And the unshaven look for men has gone just a little over the top in my opinion. It's one thing to grow a beard and keep it trimmed in an orderly fashion. It's quite another to look like you just woke up from a 3-day drunk.

I think of myself as progressive and am constantly aware that each generation has its own fashion statement and stamp of authenticity. After all, miniskirts, teased hair, clog shoes and Cleopatra eyes were my look at one time. I can only imagine what everyone thought of us back then.

Looking at the old photos, we really did look ridiculous. I even have one of me with giant hair, false eyelashes and a stupid bow right in the middle of that hair. I must have thought I was foxy enough to have my picture taken. There I was with a smug little smile looking all sassy.

What I find amusing is that as fashions change, so does my perception of them. I was so influenced by magazines that I never developed my own style. Aside from parting my hair on the left for my whole life, everything else was according to the look of the time.

Now I guess I should get my old clothes, slightly shred them, attach a bunch of junk and get with the program. I can't change the part in my hair because it's the only way I remember right from left.

Crossing the decade line

Much to my surprise, I have now crossed over from the 60's to my 70's.

It happened this summer without much ado but I think it's supposed to be significant. My body has definitely been noticing changes and my knees remind me not to run. Through the years I've learned how to modify my movements since back surgery, plowed through several attempts to control my sugar and overall seen droops and sags in unattractive places. All pretty normal stuff.

The most traumatic change came with teeth that just had to go! That process left me with great mouth health, partial apparatus and self-consciousness. I still haven't learned how to speak properly with something strange in my mouth.

When I was trying to thank my boss for a compliment and wanted to tell her she's stuck with me, it came out "Thanks. You suck." I have to work on that.

I am obviously not very modest or private about shortcomings and goings. I've earned the right to fill in the spaces, accept elastic waist pants and sliding shoulder straps.

On to memory challenges which happen at the oddest times. I'm still working and reading contracts for my job and that seems to be going well. But if you move my glasses or my ponytail band I lose it. I cannot function without them both.

At 3AM I may wake up and remember my phone isn't ringing because I forgot to disconnect the fax machine. I'm too tired so I deliberately tell myself to do it when I get up. At 9AM I'm still pacing around trying to remember what it was I forgot. The whole process goes from an "oops I forgot" to a huge chore.

Finding new things in so-called safe places when I'm cleaning can be challenging since I don't know why they're there. That decision to keep them is now based on whether it would be embarrassing for my family to find at some future date. Kind of puts things in a different perspective.

It's now the month of Thanksgiving and this holiday in particular is very special for me. As mentioned in other columns of mine, my adoption was at Thanksgiving in 1948 so I consider it my other birthday.

So whatever my flaws and signs of change might be, I am very thankful to be here with my mind intact, my body moving around and a rewarding life filled with love and friends. At this age we can say yes or no backed by years of experience and (hopefully) good judgment. It never occurs to me anything may diminish. Not today or tomorrow.

OK 70's, here I come, ready or not!

Little inconveniences

We all have little things that irritate us every day. We get used to them and find ways to either problem solve or just ignore it all.

If you have your nails done regularly, and have acrylics, you cannot pick up a coin from the floor. And you absolutely have no chance of picking up a business card either. However, if you take a business card from your desk, you can slide it under the coin on the floor.

If your hair has changed texture over the years, or a new cowlick has sprung up, no matter how much time you spend, a bad hair day is a regular thing. In fact, a good hair day is a cause for celebration.

Whatever hair style you may have had for umpteen years doesn't work anymore. If you decide to let your hair grow, you chance looking ridiculous for your age. I tried and my friends made that clear so I cut over 8" off after the summer. I had been hoping to look like those outdoors wholesome people who save trees.

Eyebrow tattoos are the only acceptable body art for some of us. It won't droop or start looking like an aging dragon hanging on our faces. But tweezing around the right shape is problematic.

Now they've introduced body sculpting for all those unwanted bulges. If you're young and you still have elasticity in your skin, you have a pretty good shot at success. If you're older and have folds from on-again off-again diets, your chances diminish greatly. I'm part of the last group so it's not an option.

And have you seen the price list for a treatment? Takes investing in your body to a whole new level!

On to body hair. I cannot speak for men (*obviously*) but after the dreaded change, I can certainly speak for women. For most of my life I've done the usual shaving in the normal places and then, without warning, the places began to change.

Hairs sprouted up out of nowhere and the places that always had them don't anymore. Go figure. I have made great friends with an electrologist because now the hairs are grey and laser can't see them. You gotta do what you gotta do.

The worst for me is the pillows under my eyes. I investigated that too and was told by a family member who is a doctor that it doesn't always produce lasting results. That was a big letdown since I actually would spend the money to get rid of them.

Now it's looking like I am what I am. Pillows, hairs, folds and all topped with perfectly manicured nails that can't pick up anything.

Professional pictures

Have you ever looked at professional photos used on business cards? Since I'm in real estate, I've had my picture taken many, many times over the years and I refuse to stand in a ¾ stance and fold my arms with a slight smile. I have pissed off many photographers to be sure.

You don't get a whole lot of posing choices and resolution is important so they tell me. I can sit at a desk, in front of a green screen and fill in the background later, look business-like with my glasses and a folder, smile sheepishly (*which never works well for me*) or just plain smile, face forward and look phony.

As you can see, I chose the face forward posed smile which my friends were quick to point out.

I wish I could use the one when I burst out laughing at my dogs or felt content on the deck of a ship at sunset. Nope. It's not professional and no business attire.

If you're in banking and mortgages, you absolutely face front, appear sincere, honest and very authoritative. After all, you're being trusted with a client's assets and looking like an idiot won't build your business.

These days whatever you do will ultimately wind up on social media.

As we all know, social media can be a very dangerous playground. Posting a vacation picture says you're not home and you can afford a vacation. Obviously you don't need to attract business with your photo.

Now social media says if you are posting for business, you must create another page specifically for that purpose. OK I'll go along with that for now.

But what do you do when your old friend of 40 years posts the one where you got drunk at Senor Frogs in Mazatlán in the 80's and everyone danced on the table singing Wooly Bully?

Either way, professional page or friend page, this is me. Dual personality and all.

I'm not sure there's a solution and once again go back in time when only important people had business cards with no pictures.

Don't mess with my soaps

Think what you will but I depend on my soap opera to reassure me that the more things change, the more they stay the same.

Forever in my memory is the first week of *General Hospital* that I watched on a small black and white TV in the girl's dorm at my boarding school. Jesse and Dr. Steve were making cow eyes at each other but ultimately he married her younger sister Audrey. And of course Jesse married the heartthrob of the story played by Roy Thinnes as Phil Brewer.

That was the early 60's and maybe the sequence is a bit off but 50-something years later their stories continue every day through multiple generations. In my opinion, all the criticism about serial dramas is misplaced. In a world of insane political antics, financial ups and downs, marriages, divorces and the uncertainty of the future, these keep going.

Every day, 5 days a week, they're loyal and don't argue with you. They don't love you but that's why we have dogs so it's not a requirement.

Sometimes it's a little hard to follow because people skip from one soap to another as in the case of a "Nina" character once on *All My Children*. Then she popped up on *One Life to Live* and now she's on *General Hospital*. I'm not sure even now where she originated or if they just had multiple Ninas but it hardly matters.

And then the stories are insane like the Cassadine crazies freezing the world only to have Luke and Laura save the planet at the last minute. Now that Luke is gone and Laura is back, the new stories are about memory transfer and cults and Laura is the mayor. Whew!

So here's the deal ladies and gentlemen. Don't mess with my soaps. They have kept me company for decades and once in a while they even take on some serious subjects quite intelligently such as harassment, cancer and bullying.

We all need constants in our lives no matter how stupid they may seem and I love my soaps!

Adjusting to inconveniences

When I broke a bone in my hand a few months ago, I learned I am a bad patient and somewhat of a control pain in the you-know-what.

Then I looked around and started to feel really selfish and stupid. Me in my pink cast and limited movement with my left hand really had nothing to complain about.

There was very little pain and my dominant hand was fine. I could still grab things here and there with my left fingers and overall nothing life threatening was going on.

It turns out I don't heal quickly so I have to learn new tricks to stay functional.

How do you squeeze out a wet washcloth? Push it with all your might against the side of the sink with your good hand and roll it around a lot.

How do you take laundry out of the dryer? Ask your husband to do it but when he's not available, lay each piece over your cast till you can hug your arm to your body and waddle to the folding table. Then go back and do it again.

Folding a sheet just isn't happening. Period. Showering with a plastic sleeve over a cast isn't too awful but it does take longer.

The real challenge is drying your hair. I bought a new hair dryer with a roller brush built in and tried that with one hand. The bristles on the brush were too soft and I have lots of hair. That was a bust.

So I balanced the old hair dryer and rolled my head around and I could use my good hand to style. It was an interesting look. I miss the days of perms when you could shower, shake and go.

Then there are dishes you can't wash, jars you can't open, groceries requiring one bag at a time, jackets that don't go over the cast, itches you can't scratch, food you can't cut, and you absolutely cannot drive a manual transmission car. Yes, we have one.

It's very humbling realizing minor inconveniences don't matter. They're just annoying.

The search is finally done!

When you're an adoptee, you learn to be patient when doing a search for birth parents. Given my age, records have been sealed for years and people who may have known about me have long since passed.

After an exhaustive search in the 80's, I found my birth mother and 2 half-brothers. It was just good old fashioned research and amateur detective work. I knew her for a few years until she died and also built a relationship with my brothers only to lose one a few years later to cancer.

I still have a relationship with my remaining brother on my mother's side, his wife and 2 children. We are on opposite sides of the county but we visit every so often.

Then along comes DNA! And best of all, it's available to ordinary people through websites, family trees and doing genetic research. Records are limited obviously because if your sibling hasn't submitted, you won't match up.

So about 4 years ago I had 2 very close matches that popped up as 1st cousins or closer and I actually met one of them. We tried and tried to figure out where the connection was but no luck. Then suddenly in January 2021, another researcher who came upon me because I am related to her husband, followed the DNA trail and discovered my entire story.

She was able to reconstruct my birth father's history down to dates and locations, marriages and children and lo and behold, my 1st cousins are actually my brother and sister. When I presented her info, my 1st cousin, now brother, confirmed that everything lined up perfectly.

My message to anyone out there searching is to never give up! Things happen in the most unexpected ways and though I would follow trails of people, I was completely off course as it turned out and they were right there in front of me.

The circle of my coming into the world is now complete in my 70's. I started getting curious in my 20's and here we are. The search is over.

Check all the boxes now

The years are piling up but my brain can't really compute that. There are so many things I vowed to do but haven't done yet because as the saying goes "Life happens while you're making other plans."

My direction has changed and so many of my old ideas of what life is supposed to be for me have been dramatically altered. Some good, some not so good but I wake up each day knowing there may be a big surprise around the next corner.

As a senior now, it can be challenging to understand that time matters. No longer the excuse of "I have 20 years to do that" or make a career change. I am what I am and I've done what I've done so now it's about that list in my head.

Spring is here and when I'm not sneezing from the new blooms, I'm feeling a bit more energized and ready for action. My body isn't always on board so changing smoke alarm batteries and filters while on a ladder isn't my best event.

What I can do, I have to do a bit slower to reach the finish line and simplify my life as much as possible. I'm giving away tons of things, desperately organizing closets, and trying to imagine what it would be like for anyone to come into this house if anything happens to me. That by itself would be a daunting task.

I go room by room opening closets and drawers cautiously and fight the instinct to keep things. That one is hard! What if it snows again? After all, no one wants to buy a 2nd snowsuit!

And friends are slipping away so I am making every effort to stay in touch but inevitably many months will go by and even though they're in my thoughts, I get distracted and forget to call.

And most importantly, new adventures are coming my way. Things I never imagined are in my path and wasting time is not an option.

So to all, start checking the boxes now and enjoy!

The beginning of me

Here we are on the back side of 2021 and my adoption history is still unfolding. I was born in 1948 in New York City when records were sealed. Birth parents had no obligation to reveal details about themselves and were excluded from knowing where their babies went the day after they were born.

Over the years I learned a few things, wandered down information roads that lead nowhere and did my best to learn what I could.

As some who have read my story know, I did find my birth mother and half-brothers in the 80's. We had a good relationship and some of the mystery of me got resolved.

Then just last year I found the other side of the story through DNA and my birth father's identity was revealed. And suddenly there were siblings there too welcoming me.

I'm one of the lucky ones. I've learned so much about how things were 70 years ago and the back stories are so interesting. But I say I'm lucky also because I had not been part of a very chaotic time in my birth family's life. I'm grateful they have welcomed me now so many years later even though both birth parents are gone.

So why do I say that only now did I find "the beginning of me?"

My original birth certificate has just arrived and I opened the envelope to see the time, place, name, labor hours, etc. One piece of paper in my hand suddenly puts reality in focus.

I was stunned and speechless staring at it.

I can close the book on this because I now have everything there is to find. As states unseal their records, we adoptees finally have the right to know how we got here and why. You spend your whole life accepting secrecy because that's the way it was.

I never felt resentment and I was raised by loving parents but certain facts were withheld all my life and decisions were made that I could not contest. Now we have a chance to come full circle and learn how we began.

Doing my happy dance

The older we get, the crankier some of us are. Add to that the whining, complaining and sharing of medical horror stories and every little inconvenience becomes a major event.

Some have reasons and some don't. But what's so funny about the whole routine is that we have endless conversations about our issues big and small. No one objects to hearing and sometimes one of us yells "I win" as one story tops the other.

So what do you do when you're happy? When the time comes that you've moved on from sadness and loss, the light shines brighter and life is just better. New people come along, new bonds are formed and things seem to stabilize.

I had no idea how annoying I sound to my friends when I tell them how happy I am these days.

Some friends never know what to do with "happy!" There's nothing to talk about.

All the aches and pains are still there, and the doctor visits go on, but I really don't dwell on anything. They're no longer the center of my world. I limp or take an extra moment to get my hip to work but it's kind of 2nd nature now.

At a time in our history when we are witness to so much devastation and suffering, I appreciate more than ever how tranquil my life really is. I have a lovely roof over my head, food when I want it, precious pets, and all the necessities to be comfortable and the ability to make choices for myself.

We take our comfort for granted most of the time but it is clear today that I should celebrate where I am. If my arthritis decides to act up more than normal, get the heating pad and shut up. The same is true for the old lady that stares at me from the mirror. It doesn't matter.

Every time I ask my dogs if they want dinner, they dance around the kitchen wagging tails and knocking each other over. Now I dance the happy dance with them!

Involuntary moves

Lately I've been noticing that my body makes movement decisions without my consent. That can be very annoying and each time it happens, I just concentrate on undoing it.

In theory, the conscious acknowledgment of the issue should work but, alas, it isn't so.

Here's an example: When you hold the mouse for your computer, your index finger pretty much directs the motion. Your ring finger just rests on the side of the mouse and your thumb just pushes everything around. Your pinky just hangs around and scrapes the pad.

But what about the middle finger? It never cooperates and lays down flat. It has no job to do so it starts pointing up. I try every which way to get it to rest down but it doesn't want to do that.

Do you suppose it's secretly giving my computer the bird? That's probably it.

Moving on to knees. They have survived falls, scrapes and hard work carting around the rest of me. They're tough but everything has a shelf life and they rebel by just plain buckling in the middle of walking. No warning. I've tuned in to their bad behavior so I try to act prepared in public by moving very carefully. I suspect knee replacement is right around the corner.

Twitching is a new one for me. With all the wind, allergens and air pollutants, my eyes involuntarily squint and try to clear up things. That has evolved into defensive twitches and looks really weird. And, as my eyes change, I can squint driving when headlights come at me. Not pretty. In the old days I could drive at night with floodlights in my face but no more.

The other twitches are simply muscle movements in odd places. My shoulder and neck have an uncontrollable desire to stretch for no reason. It can be jerky or subtle and it's always a surprise. There's nothing wrong with me and I've driven my doctor crazy with questions.

As I notice these things, I take it in stride and adjust to my new normal. I'm still me.

Quite by chance

In this world of the internet and DNA connections, I was able to find my birth family in my 70's. Not something I would have expected but certainly something I celebrate as I learn my genetic history. I've been very lucky because they all accept me as I am, send photos and we keep in touch.

As an adoptee, it never occurred to me that a link would be found for my adoptive parents that included me. And so it happened that I showed up as their daughter on someone else's search and voila! There are people everywhere from my mom's side and what a colorful bunch they are!

I remember my grandmother and my uncle. They both were very intimidating to a little girl. The family background is Russian and their demeanors were rough and scary. When my grandmother would visit, I would go to my room and play until she left. When my uncle bought me gifts, they were for a little boy instead of a girl. Not sure what that was all about.

My great uncle was a dentist in the days of old drills. That pain resonates with me even now. I still hate dentists.

So here we are in 2022 and a cousin contacts me out of the blue. As we explore all these connections, I was able to contribute some memories of people and places as a child and now we've even done zoom calls comparing stories.

The real story has emerged as a historic tale of immigrants escaping Russia, marriages and adventures both painful and exhilarating. One cousin has collected notes and diaries to be assembled sometime in the future for us all.

When New York opened its birth records a few years ago, I thought that was it. I got my original birth certificate. Even though I already found my birth mother, I still was stunned to see the actual document of my birth. Now this whole other side has opened up.

These are amazing times so I guess my story goes on a while longer. Stay tuned!

Groping. It's not what you think!

When we were younger, groping was considered offensive or welcoming depending on who did it. A little pat here, a stroke there or a quick grab from your intimate partner was a nice little surprise.

As seniors, physical groping works differently! We have to reach lower and be a little gentler, no sudden springing upon us and a zealous pat could knock us over.

Enter a new form of groping for words! We engage in serious conversations and have something very important to say. No words come out. That's senior groping.

It can take me 2 minutes or more in real time to find the right word and even then, it doesn't always go the way I want. I make up words and combine 2 other words to make a new one in the hope someone will understand me.

So while we're on the subject of processing information, how about asking a question? I have been known to ask the same question at least a dozen times just to be sure I got that right. That's the thinking grope.

There's no instant recall in my brain of what someone said so it's better to annoy them with a repeat question. The answer is usually said with great emphasis and a reminder we've already talked about it.

And how many times have I told the same story? This part may not qualify as groping but it's kind of a reverse thing. For some reason, known only to my inner self, I need to make sure everyone has heard my tales. Perhaps it's a little disorder of all seniors but the good side is that when friends do that to me, it might sound new again.

Lots of us spend a lot of time in this space. I liken it to those where the character wakes up to no memory of the day before. Every day is a new challenge and keeps us on our toes, so grope away, my friends!

Senior beauty checklist

Yes, I'm back into checklists for seniors because every time I turn around, there's some new thing I have to do in the labored effort to be the best I can be.

Success is never guaranteed of course but I have new challenges with my appearance in my 70's. I have a multitude of professionals who help me along in ways I never imagined 20 years ago.

I stopped wearing make-up about 30 years ago. All the fancy lotions and even hemorrhoid creams disguised as expensive formulas do not work and here I am. I did eyebrow tatoos as a solution to not looking like a ghost.

So I look in the mirror and I have eye pillows, laugh lines, crows feet and my eyelids are a bit droopy. All of that can be fixed with plastic surgery if I wanted to risk looking like a dolphin when it's done. I hear there's a Botox treatment that can help but I haven't had the nerve to try it.

How about those arms! My batwings jiggle when I shake a jar so I hide in a corner of the kitchen whenever that happens.

And after losing weight, the fold would mean a tummy tuck and I hate pain.

Legs that once modeled pantyhose (Remember those?) now look unrecognizable to me. Knee problems lead to injections and physical therapy in a futile effort to postpone knee surgery. So far, I'm winning.

Haircuts are big decisions. We think of ourselves as we once were. It used to be we resisted cutting our hair shorter in an effort to maintain our youthful appearance. There's that defining moment when you realize you don't look the part anymore and your image needs a makeover. I cried as I watched my hair hit the floor. OMG! Now everyone can see my neck!

When I think about taking drastic measures to look younger, I realize that time is not on my side. I will not waste a year of my life getting cut and then healed when every day is so valuable as we age.

Fireflies & worms

If you were a city girl, chances were that either your family or a friend's family had a country house for the summers. And, if you were lucky, your Mom and Dad knew all the fun things to do outdoors since there was a no TV back there.

Our country house had a screened-in porch with 2 rockers and Daddy would sit out there and read every afternoon. Of course we went to the small store at the end of the road for treats and the paper each morning too. You could listen to the rustling leaves and enjoy the light breezes coming through the screens.

I created my own world on the side of the house between 2 full grown pine trees. I could crawl in and pretend it was a cave, sit in pine needles and play with pinecones. Sometimes I brought my dolls out there for a party.

I even had a little tin swimming pool and all the neighbors' kids were naked.

We also found a duckling on the road who had been separated from the mother so we took her in and raised her in the bathtub until she was old enough to go to a friend's farm. They had white swans so imagine our surprise when she developed and it turned out she was a he with the most beautiful iridescent feathers we ever saw! He went on to rule that farm.

We had a brook behind the property and you could fish there too. My mother was a real country girl when we were there. She could make a fishing line and hook, dig out worms and climb trees to throw out the line. Back then I didn't mind worms.

But the best evenings were taking empty jars down a dark road and catching fireflies. We would run and run until the jar was full and bring them back to light up the porch.

Childhood summers were innocent and years later I went back and my pine trees were gone. But memories of fireflies, worms and tranquility stay with me.

Dogs Rule

Life is different without the big red dog

In mid-July we lost our Golden Retriever to old age. Born with hip problems, he was never expected to have a long life. At 8 weeks he weighed 11 pounds so we all knew he would be big.

He made it 2 months shy of 14 and had puppy moments until the day he stroked. As an adult dog, he weighed in at 125 pounds, was a genuine pool puppy, could throw and retrieve his own toys and never had a bad day.

I think Goldens hold the key to happiness and spread it around everyone who gets near. They exude calm by tuning into your every thought. Since he was my first Golden, I was amazed at how smart, creative, sensitive and playful he was his whole life.

When he went to the pet sitter, he opened all the doors and let everyone run around. He did it at the groomer too. I think he considered it his job.

He watched everything we did and copied it.

The big red dog would get water from the water cooler by pressing down on the lever. We finally asked Sparkletts to install childproof levers because the kitchen floor kept getting flooded.

Ever curious, he once got his head stuck in a vase and suddenly he was flat out on the rug, frozen in place. The instant my hand touched him, he relaxed and I pulled him out. We laughed til we cried.

If I was planning a trip, I dropped him at the sitter before packing. If anyone even moved a piece of luggage in the house, he would start dancing around and running to the door. This would go on for hours!

We learned to pile clothes in hidden places, ready to pack, hoping to fool him until the last possible minute. Since he usually went with us, he wouldn't calm down until he was in the car.

We've taken care of other people's dogs and he never objected. He shared his toys, let them sleep on him and steal his place on the couch. I sure wish humans were that gracious!

It's hard walking around the house now. He would strategically place himself right in your path to make sure he got a cookie, a pat on the head or a hug. All the walkways in the house are clear. It feels empty.

Before we were married, my husband worked in Lake Havasu so we commuted a lot. Stopping to use a restroom, too hot to leave him in the car, I wrapped his feet and took him with me. I wasn't about to let him get unknown public bathroom germs so he pretended to be a service dog.

The lake beach allowed dogs so we put him on a 50-foot lead and let him retrieve toys. With a life vest to help, he would swim & swim & swim!

Getting him back out was near impossible! He would come to shore and sit down. Have you ever tried to move a 125-pound wet dog in sand?

Finally coaxing him to the grassy area, we collapsed on a blanket exhausted while the big drippy dog watched over us.

Thank you for giving us everything you had. We miss you.

Louie

In my day job, I am a real estate Broker Associate. I've been at it for a pretty long time and even with the vast market changes and job responsibilities, not much shocks me. But nothing prepared me for what I stumbled upon at the height of the foreclosure crisis.

On many occasions, and I do mean many, I would open a door to show an abandoned vacant house only to find pets locked up inside with no food or water. The houses would have unbearable smells and filth. Somewhere, crunched in a corner or a closet, we would find a terrified, starving cat or dog.

People were actually just abandoning their family pets in locked houses. If this had been a one-time incident, I wouldn't be writing about it. It happened time and time again.

Many real estate agents saved hundreds of animals over these last years and then a new non-profit formed called "Foreclosed Upon Pets" which grew to rescue thousands of dogs and cats.

If you recall my column last summer, we lost our big golden retriever. The time came to adopt in the fall. With so many beautiful dogs available, it was hard to choose until my husband saw this little guy on the FUPI website and started making calls.

Enter Louie! He had a cone on his head because of an infection that was being treated but they agreed to bring him to an adoption event for us to be introduced. We packed up our other dog and off we went.

It was instant love. He wasn't afraid of us, snuggled down in our laps, socialized beautifully and we were hooked.

He's about 3 or 4 years old and no one knows exactly what he is. His coloring is all messed up and he has no pigment around one eye with white eyelashes. The other eye looks like someone socked him or drew magic marker around it. The under bite just adds to the cuteness.

Louie's been with us about 4 months now. He has crazy teenage moments and goes running around at lightning speed a few times a day. He absolutely loves toys and knows to put them away in a basket. He doesn't like the rain so we have a few housebreaking issues on stormy days. Oh well.

We think he may have been a runner because one day I accepted a delivery and he flew past me and down the street. I chased him, stopped traffic and got him back safely. He's getting a little training in that department too.

He's a bed hog. Not much we can do about that so we've adjusted.

When you give this dog a hug, he gets very relaxed and lays his head on your shoulder.

Our Shih Tzu now thinks he's a sheepherder and makes every attempt to get Louie to do what he wants. They chase each other so you have to be careful where you walk in case flying dogs are present.

Now the Barrera household is a little more fun again. There's probably room for another so we're keeping that door open.

Have a great New Year everyone!

My dogs love me more than I love them?

Have you ever thought about dog love and loyalty in terms of human behavior versus dog admiration and acceptance?

Dogs have no animosity and no preconceived notions about the future. They look at every moment with joy and optimism, jumping up and down happily when an adventure is about to begin.

Their at-home habits are all about comfort and pleasing you. They guard territory, are couch potatoes, follow orders, have play time and nap time, exercise, obey and have their own bathroom with the only difference being it's outside in the yard. They are potty trained like children and bribed with treats.

So after all this obedience, you would think they could rely on us to honor their wishes and eat at the same time every day, not be left alone too long and give them the full run of just about everything.

Nope. It doesn't work that way. We take them for granted because they're so good.

When I'm working at home, I usually have 2 little faces staring up at me trying to communicate. I let them out, give them treats and sometimes they come back and continue to stare.

Then the talking starts. One makes these silly noises in dog talk and turns his head to the side. I have absolutely no idea what he wants so I say "Show me" and he just stands there. The other one just waits patiently with this soulful look focused on my every move.

We try going out, fresh water, the treat and cuddle thing a few more times and finally everyone gives up and they let out a sigh of pure frustration and lie down. I know they're bitterly disappointed but I have no idea why.

Imagine if dogs were the caregivers and we had to sit in the dark waiting for them to come home to feed us? We know the dish is on the counter, the food is in the pantry and the water faucet is up there somewhere too. We just can't reach it!

No one meant to leave us alone that long and maybe they got a phone call or went shopping and lost track of time. Either way, we're stuck at floor level, hungry and in the dark.

What about that housebreaking thing? Just how long do they

think we can wait? We had a treat from the table and it totally upset our tummies but we still have to wait. Then if we try to find a corner of the human bathroom before bursting, they get mad at us and still put us out.

It's a never-ending cycle of miscommunication. In our neighborhood we can't leave dog doors open because of coyotes and other critters.

But no matter how late we are coming home, and even when we get mad at them for chewing a favorite shoe, they forgive us and are overwhelmed with joy when we arrive. I cannot imagine a love so pure as that which dogs have for their masters. All is overshadowed by affection and loyalty.

I wish I could forget bad days and learn to love as purely as our dogs love us. It's certainly something to keep striving for no matter what age you are.

Old person with small dogs

You may wonder who I am referring to with the title so let me clear it up right now. I am the old person with a small dog. Now no one needs to be insulted and we move right along.

All the years of pets have always included a big, huggable horse of a dog. You can roll around with them, play Frisbee or chase tennis balls. Big dogs are always easy to find and seldom succeed at hiding after eating the couch or chewing a hole in the drywall.

I love big dogs. Period.

So now I have 2 little dogs and for the life of me I can't explain how that happened. They're quick and smart and rule our home wielding more power than any big dog.

One in particular, Tyler, bosses us around but it's hard to argue with him. He hates raised voices so if we have a misunderstanding, he lets us have it. In fact, he is so defiant, we have to continue the conversation in calm, monotone voices or he will throw a barking fit. He should get his therapist license.

The other one, Louie, is our rescue boy and not much upsets him. He has a laissez faire attitude most of the time. If you open the back door, he will either go out and inspect the perimeter or sit on the rug just inside and watch for invaders.

He is also a runner. He has absolutely no fear and tears out through any opening, flies down the street and inspects everything. Most rescues are happy to have a home and rarely like to leave. But not our boy! You never know if he's going to guard the castle or go exploring.

I think he's overly secure so a few side trips here and there are no big deal. And he's small so grabbing him as he flees the door is out of the question. Now we go in and out of our home as though we're in a secure lab with multiple doors.

Next come the grooming issues. With big dogs like shepherds and labs, you just have to bathe them and brush once in a while. Our Golden required grooming a few times a year but overall, big dogs are easy. My hat's off to owners with sheepdogs, collies and long-hairs however I've had no experience with that.

Here comes the Shih Tzu brigade with silky coats that grow

overnight. Louie may have some poodle so his fur is soft and then he sprouts curls. We did his DNA test and there's 1/8th something that could be poodle or bulldog. Not too sure about that.

Tyler is pure Shih Tzu so brushing him is mandatory if he allows it. Pet his tummy and we're good. Bring out the brush and it's questionable.

So why do we have small dogs? Because they tug at your heart by just looking at you. They're portable which is great because you never want to leave them. They sleep by your side no matter what and make you talk stupid.

The little ones have taken over our lives. And best of all, they fit just about anywhere.

Love & care of senior dogs

With all the talk of loving support from friends and neighbors as we age, we don't usually consider how our pets age. They can sometimes be surrendered to rescues when someone is ill or worse yet, their owners pass away and family members don't want them.

When we lost our golden retriever 3 years ago, I missed having a big red dog to trip over. The thought of adopting another was overwhelming because at our ages, we couldn't take on a puppy or a 100-pound 2-year-old. That would be too much!

I did some investigating about older dogs and found that some rescue organizations have foster families that take in sick, injured or older dogs so they can live their senior years in comfort.

These dogs, through unfortunate circumstances, are loving, gentle companions. The unconditional loyalty and love they offer is calming. Dogs know when you're trying to help them and let you know how appreciated you are. Their communication skills are amazing.

With one look, a raised ear, a soulful stare or any small expression change, a dog can tell you how he feels, what he wants and what he expects from you.

Dogs have patience and can wait however long it takes for you to respond to them. They pace themselves to your speed so you never feel pressure. Even when they're displaced, they wait to see what's next.

We were feeling the void of not having a big dog. We still instinctively looked around corners to make sure we wouldn't trip over one even though it had been 3 years since ours had passed.

So we started the search for an older dog and within a few months, we got the call. Golden Retriever Rescue of Southern Nevada was about to take in 3 senior goldens, all from the same home needing care. We were so excited to get the call and made arrangements to meet the next day.

We wanted a smaller golden, about 60 to 70 lbs., and along came this beautiful boy. He was 112 lbs., has a rod in his leg, is 10 years old and is not at all aggressive. We had our 2 little ones with us to meet and greet and that went well.

He loves the car and sat in the back with his head draped over my husband's shoulder all the way home. It took him about 2 weeks to understand what was happening and then he began playing with his toys.

His tail can knock over furniture when he wags and things in the Barrera household are normal again.

Most importantly, this experience reminds us how rewarding it can be to take in a senior dog. No matter why they are abandoned, they are lost and need love.

Whether you love retrievers, poodles, shepherds or mutts, think about how much better life can be with one of these beautiful seniors. Call your favorite rescue and check out the possibilities!

The great grape incident

This month's title refers to a specific evening but to be more explicit, I am writing about what not to feed your pets during this holiday season of treats and goodies.

A few weeks ago, on a Friday night, I was carrying a plate of white seedless grapes to the couch to munch on watching TV. I piled too many in the dish and some rolled off to the floor.

Everything happened so fast at that point that I barely got to pick up what I thought was only 4 or 5 grapes. I grabbed them immediately but realized the 13-pound Shih Tzu had something in his mouth and would not give it up. He growled when I tried to open his jaw.

Then I looked at the other one, Louie, and he was just waiting for more to drop.

Knowing in the back of my mind I read that grapes and raisins are bad for dogs, I looked it up on the computer and found out my dogs could actually die from it.

Our vet had late hours that evening and I almost ran red lights getting there with two stunned dogs. They induced vomiting and found that Louie had eaten 3 big grapes and Tyler had crushed one. This is the one time I was glad that Louie inhales his food because they were still whole!

My poor dogs had no idea what hit them but thank goodness our vet handled the situation before anything was fully digested.

Now I have a list of foods that can be poisonous to pets and I would like to share it with you this holiday season. We don't always think about how their systems are different from ours and you may be surprised at a few of these.

This list is taken from the Humane Society website and for more information, you can also google many other sources. In alphabetical order, they are:

Alcoholic Beverages, Apple Seeds, Apricot Pits, Avocados, Cherry Pits, Candy (particularly chocolate and any candy containing the toxic sweetener Xylitol) Coffee and chocolate-covered espresso beans, Garlic, Grapes, Gum can cause blockages and contain artificial sweetener, Hops, Macadamia Nuts, Moldy Foods or

Mushroom Plants, Mustard Seeds, Onions and Onion Powder, Peach Pits, Potato Leaves & Stems (green part), Raisins, Rhubarb Leaves, Salt, Tea because it contains caffeine, Tomato Leaves & Stems, Walnuts, Xylitol which is toxic to pets and Yeast Dough.

There are additional sites that provide more extensive lists so I urge everyone to watch all that holiday candy and avoid people food treats for your pets. Even little kids with candy canes can innocently poison your pet.

It only takes one mistake and a small dog's kidneys could shut down or they become lethargic and sick.

In our house, Superman has nothing on our Louie when it comes to moving "faster than a speeding bullet" if there's food involved. He must get that from me.

Wishing everyone a holiday season filled with love and happiness!

Notes to the neighborhood

The lifestyle in an age-restricted neighborhood brings with it a unique set of rules. We enjoy the quiet, uneventful days and slow pace of not having to run after kids on bikes, telling teenagers not to screech the tires and overall empty nest living.

And then we become very judgmental about things that would never have bothered us before. For example, anyone thinking of planting another mesquite with yellow flowers should move. Those sticky, dried up ugly droppings should be banned. At the very least, people who have them should pay the landscaping bills for their neighbors. If you're a carpet person, be prepared for yellow stains too.

In the evenings, when all the little dogs go out for their walks, thank you for picking up after them as they mark territory in front of my house. As for the big ones, bring several garbage bags. You need them and so do we.

The delinquents of the neighborhood are the bunnies. We have the most resourceful rabbits in the area. They can actually eat fences, flower guards, ground cover repellent and plants that are listed as rabbit-resistant.

On our 4th try of deterrents, we found a mix of herb based ground cover that they supposedly don't like. Told that anything with a strong odor will keep them away, we bought $40 worth of the stuff, spread it around and much to our surprise, there they were enjoying a flower meal in our back yard anyway.

I actually drove the neighborhood to see what others are doing and I'm convinced that rabbits leave front yards alone. Even if I put in the same fences, if it's in the back yard they call their little bunny buddies and develop a strategy to get around it.

Nobody sees this but I'm sure they have a secret life like Gary Larsen's cows. (Hopefully you remember the cows of years ago.)

What has worked is to plant some wild flowers in the middle of rosemary. And it smells nice after a rain.

The only offenders are people who feed coyotes. I really wish they could be held responsible for all the pets that have been attacked because people leave food for them. Yes, they're displaced from their natural habitat and come looking for food. But these stupid people don't think about the danger to others. For heaven's sake, *don't feed the coyotes!* We want our pets to be safe.

All things considered, age-restricted communities are pretty cool.

Some assembly required

Just when you think the days of putting together toys and household items has gone by, the internet orders have taken over and the words "Some Assembly Required" appear on everything.

You can call someone to come to your home and put things together, or you can go to a store and pay extra for the same guy to do it there, or just try it yourself.

All the savings of the sale just get eaten up by assembly fees so we decided we were smart enough to do it.

Let's take the new dog stroller to start. The sales price was reduced and seemed like a great deal with over $150 savings. *Quel surprise!*

The size looked about the same but when the box came, the thing was huge and it had giant wheels, axle and some other miscellaneous parts to connect. I could fit our old one into this one but we decided the dogs would love having more room to look around so we'll keep it.

First lesson learned is that most things are not American made even if you didn't notice that when you ordered. So be prepared to read the loose translation of instructions with thumbnail sized pictures you can't see.

My husband figured it out and I just stood there confused. Say what you will about women doing anything and everything, I am not one of them.

Then there was a headboard in exactly the color and style I wanted. Got a great price on that too. So when all the rails, screws, washers, bolts and hardware came, I was on a mission and after 2 days, I got it.

As for the little storage shed in the yard, the weather had to be just right or the plastic wouldn't fit together.

Personally I would be willing to pay for a bigger box to get it all put together but sadly, no one offers that. Now when I order something, I block out a chunk of time for translations, enlarging the diagrams and hoping I don't injure myself along the way.

Getting a new bed

It's a new year and we're guilty of resolutions never kept from the year before. More concentrated effort is promised for this year but not much changes. We go through the same old promises of diets, budgets and closet cleaning.

So we made a bold move and decided to buy a new bed.

There are all sorts of warnings about new beds, when and why to buy them, how healthy or not healthy they are after a few years and prices that are so confusing you might want to just keep sleeping on the old one another 10 years.

The first serious discussion was the size of the bed. Can we manage a queen with 2 dogs that get first right of position every night? The king crowded the bedroom so my choice was to scale down a little. I figured the dogs would have to adjust. After all, they're dogs!

Then came the new headboard and whether or not to hang something over our heads on the wall. Coming from earthquake country, I have a thing about things over my head while I'm asleep. Been there, done that.

But I was ready to compromise and buy a tapestry for the wall. Not a big one but just enough so it didn't look bare. It's 23" X 54" and looks awesome in great jewel tones. I forgot one thing. It hangs on a curtain rod affixed to the wall and if that comes down on my head, I'm not going to be happy. So much for my great idea.

New colors on the tapestry call for new colors on the bed. We have a new comforter, sheet sets, euro-pillow covers, and shams with a new side rug by the bed. Not sure I saved anything.

The bed goes up and down at the head & the foot. We never agree on which way we really like it and one night the puppies slid down the pillow because the head was too high. I wound up with a tail in my eye.

We're getting used to it.

Me & my boys

Never one to miss an opportunity to talk about my boys, last year was especially hard and they have been a pure joy for me.

I have the responsibility to care for them so when I'm feeling blue, I look at those magical faces and do something for them. No matter what, they are total wag-a-dogs and love all the attention.

Dogs transcend logic. They have abilities we don't understand and sometimes I think they are clearly more evolved than us mere humans. Their sensitivity and perceptions are pure and they define unconditional love.

And when they are having a day of stubborn independence, they make me laugh out loud. They know and I know that eventually I will win because I am the pack leader. But that doesn't matter because they will stretch out the moment as long as they can like petulant children.

Expert at learning routines, these little guys can manipulate the moment any time they choose. If they want a treat, one stands at the door to go out first. They go out to do their business and circle back in knowing a treat is on its way. I'm on to it and most of the time there's no business to be done but they're too cute to deny.

Since one had been a service dog for my husband, we go everywhere. They have even been on cruises, to out of town casino hotels and resorts. I will say that going to a specific place on a ship to poop is interesting. It's a huge kitty litter box and they want nothing to do with it! But we worked it out.

The fun part on the cruise was when one had his picture taken and people wanted to buy it before I ever saw it. Some ladies gave us the heads up at breakfast so I ran to the gallery.

Just before Thanksgiving I took them for a photo shoot from a gift certificate I received. They posed like they had done it a million times before and here we are.

Golden alert!

When the world lost Betty White, quotes and interviews were playing all over social media and TV. An animal advocate and beloved star with a huge heart said her parents were great animal lovers and her love began at an early age.

Of her quotes, my favorite is from 2009: "You don't meet a golden retriever and go home to think about it."

We totally understand. Every breed has a quality that makes them irresistible but to explain a golden is like trying to explain magic. Goldens exude love, admiration and loyalty by just being. You can't explain it in words because no one gesture or look defines them.

An old calendar quote by Ann Landers hangs on my refrigerator and says, "Don't accept your dog's admiration as conclusive evidence that you are wonderful." And that's the truth! It has a picture of a golden.

We have a new rescue named Ginger. How anyone could have given her up is beyond me but she's ours now. My imperfections and bad attitude days don't seem to matter to her.

She's a pain in the butt at 5AM she wants to play and dumps her toy on my face, jumps on the bed and makes it clear she's ready for the day. They say she's 3 but we think she's a bit younger.

So in the evening when all is calm in the house, she lays down with a big stuffed toy in her mouth and sleeps. I've tried explaining that she can skip her afternoon naps and that way she'll sleep through the night but alas, no such luck.

She runs like a racehorse at the park and leaps over any obstacle with no hesitation. She also tries to engage the 2 Shih Tzus at home but only manages to trample them. They put up with it and get out of the way when she does the zoomies.

She's a licker too. You can't avoid it. It's supposedly a sign of love and submissiveness but I think she's actually the one in charge. You can't resist that face!

The dog yard

I remember the days when I had a huge back yard, a pool, a casita, trees, and grass with rose bushes everywhere. I even had too many trees and was always trimming them away from the house. Personally, I don't think you can ever have too many trees.

So now life is different. It's simple, minimal maintenance and designed to please the dogs.

Dogs have their own agenda when they go into the yard. First, they have to check the perimeter and make sure there are no monsters hiding in the bushes and then they're off to their favorite poop spot.

I've come to predict where they'll go and I plan around it. Luckily, it's off in the back corners. The little ones on the left and the big one on the right.

I trimmed all the trees at the bottom so there are no coyote hiding spots but now I have a clear view of their bathroom. Fair exchange, I guess.

Next is the plan. Whatever I do back there has to be dog proof and cannot invade their space. I thought as I got older, I had rights but alas, that's not the case.

We got the Golden a small pool for the summer so that has to have a designated spot. We also need to sit and be able to visit with people without them getting the shake after the swim.

Then we have to consider that the small dogs don't like water and need a safe spot. They bark at everything too so visibility must be limited for them.

We're down to pavers now so everything can be hosed down and dirt doesn't fly around as much. I am hoping they don't all decide that pavers are a good bathroom.

After all this, they're actually house dogs. I never leave them outside without supervision because of the obvious coyote risks. So all this planning is for their few minutes several times a day and when someone is there.

This may all sound silly but if you're a dog lover, you'll do it too.

A Little Romance

The internet bar scene

Being single again can be overwhelming, but add this new internet method of meeting people and the idea sends shockwaves. For a person who thinks too much as it is, this scene is a disaster for the mind.

I went on a dating site and entered a new orbit. Everything I knew had changed. Remember when Friday was singles night and Saturday was date night? Not now. So how do you step into this new world?

When I was part of a couple, I never thought twice about complimenting a man on his work or attitude. Maybe we shared an interest and I wanted to speak to him. A phone call wasn't out of the question when I was part of a couple. As single, it's considered flirting.

I get my first email on the site and I answer. Nothing. I answer someone again, we say a few things and although our styles are not the same, it's a nice, polite exchange and everyone moves along. That's good.

There were some who sent a "wink." An electronic wink is the way to flirt in high tech talk. Who knew?

Why would someone 2,000 miles away email me? Then a local man made his intentions quite clear in a polite sort of way. Gotta hand it to him, he cut right to it! I hope he finds what he's looking for. That age gap was 23 years and probably would have injured me.

Then I get noticed by a very interesting person and I'm a deer in headlights. Do I answer? How about that wink thing? What should be a normal, calm introduction has turned to brain chaos. Reading his page he seems smart, arrogant and fun. He either has a fabulous sense of humor or is just arrogant and smart.

I look again at his profile. Great big smile, silver hair, dress shirt and tie. Probably an office photo. He lives about 150 miles away. That seems safe enough. No risk of running into him. He started it so I reply.

Now I'm nervous, bouncing around like I'm 20 and wondering if he's that good guy. None of my thoughts are connected. Every paranoid emotion I may have ever had has now risen to the surface. We're talking about an email for goodness sake! How stupid is that?

You never forget that uneasy feeling when meeting someone new. While my mind was on spin cycle, it never occurred to me I might not like him. Ever had the feeling the world just has to like you or you'll fold up? Forget being 20. I'm 12 and I have issues.

My profile was pretty straight forward. No mention of moonlit beach walks or candlelight. I put myself on a path for a what-you-see-is-what-you-get kind of match. At 60 you get to do that. The beauty of being 60 is you probably won't be changing, you get to say no and the diet is on the back burner for now.

My reply said he could probably run circles around me. His reply? "Are you up to the challenge?" I laughed out loud, by myself, knowing he had read me pretty well. This was going to be fun!

To be continued.....

Online dating, continued

Recently I was drafting a talk on senior internet dating since I had met my husband that way over 6 years ago. So I accessed a website to see what might have changed since 2009.

This time I didn't sign up but instead I "browsed" the site with initials as ID and an email. There is no profile on me. I get 24 possible dates every day meeting my criteria that doesn't exist. They say many have viewed my profile. What profile?

I looked at these hot prospects and wondered if they were serious or just plain distasteful. No shirt over 65 just doesn't get my attention no matter how much he thinks it does. Even movie stars don't reveal all over 65. Let us fall for you first so we won't judge.

Sorry if that sounds a little bitchy but I certainly wouldn't post me in a bathing suit either. You absolutely have to be crazy in love with me first!

Other candidates were slouched in chairs but apparently exercise 4 to 6 times a week. They might want to adopt a different routine because clearly it's not working.

One of my personal favorites was a shorter man who described himself as having "a few extra pounds" and wants a slender woman. Maybe he's trying to split the difference?

Many are much older and want athletic, toned women 40 to 50 years old. Is there money involved? Is this short term?

On the more genuine side are real people writing of simple interests and a level of maturity that comes through their profiles. They're careful with personal information, but through the writing one can notice modesty and humor. And you can read between the lines and see education in the mix.

It's very hard to find that balance between age acceptance and appreciation with a bright attitude. Any illusion, or delusion, will be quickly reduced on your first meeting.

The laughter, interests, beliefs, past life and accomplishments are part of the bundle and we should wear them proudly. However we arrived at this point has to count for something.

Except for personal introductions, interest clubs and the workplace, you're invariably stuck with internet dating sites. They offer so many varieties that it's very confusing. It's a big fishing expedition.

Christian sites go one way and adulterers go another. And speaking of fish, there's actually one called "Plenty of Fish!" How imaginative. There are hundreds of sites for just about anything you want in a mate.

The way it works now, as opposed to 6 years ago, looks different. I think the internet dating world has finally reached a maximum load capacity. When I gave it a shot, there was Match.com. I looked around for a few days and he accidentally found me. I got lucky.

I caution anyone these days to take time, look at the free trials and pick a site that seems to have members you find appealing & interesting. Be careful with your information and never forget it's public.

If you're looking, it's as good a place as any. For men and women alike, this stuff can become toxic if you're not selective. It can also have a fairy tale ending.

From the Internet Dating Site to *Great Expectations!*

A few months ago I wrote about my initiation to internet dating. February is Valentine's month so my story continues.

We made contact! Suddenly there was a voice, a slight east coast accent mixed with some other something I couldn't quite figure out and a slow, raspy, friendly sound. This was a grown-up!

After all the stories and misadventures of friends, I was naturally cautious. We exchanged the who, what, where and why of how we wound up on the internet. I paid very close attention hoping for a moment of great discovery. A bit dramatic but I was ready for drama. It was time for a good story to happen in my life.

The discovery moment didn't happen as planned. It was more like a conversation between friends. We talked about our interests, our favorite accomplishments and motivations. Coincidentally, as kids we lived 6 blocks from each other so I asked if he was ever run over by a 10-year-old on a blue bike. He didn't recall.

We spoke 3 evenings in a row for 3 hours each time. He was an accomplished professional, divorced, working in another state and planning for a full retirement I was filled with idiotic questions and he, the gentleman, answered each one patiently with explanations I could understand. By the end of the 3rd day, he planned a trip to Las Vegas.

From the beginning, my instincts told me he would play a role in my life. We had connected in a very fun, respectful and gentle way. With so many unknowns, I was strangely comfortable.

In other writings I've said that at 60 you get to tell the facts and not embellish quite as much about how you look, what you weigh and your age. I saw posted photos of people I knew that were taken 20 years ago. What were they thinking?

Our lives are filled with adventure stories of years past, families, points of view, habits both good and bad. If you don't have any baggage at 60, what did you do all those years? Everybody comes with "stuff."

I wanted to meet someone for dinner or have a companion at social gatherings. I wanted a person to converse with about my work, his work and goals. The so-called "bucket list" that I have yet to write includes new places I've never been or stepping out of my norm into someone else's favorite place. There might be some limitations on that one. We'll see.

Being older & dating is a very scary thing. Your mind is fine, or at least YOU think it is. Making contact with a new person can be whatever you want it to be. At our age, intuition can be more reliable than when we were 20. I wanted to hear what another person had to say, express myself in a very direct manner and share the task of drawing new life pictures on a clean canvas.

My search to step out again was starting out well. My dog even told me not to mess this up.

Fast forward 3 years and I married him.

Marriage casting

Have you ever charted the roles we play over the life of a marriage? While out to dinner with friends, they noted how some things reverse the longer they're married as each gives up the leadership in certain areas.

Let's take going out to dinner as a prime example. She reads the menu and he looks at her wondering what it was that he likes. Finally annoyed at having to go through pages of food choices he says "What do I want for dinner?" She tells him and he's relieved he doesn't have to make a decision.

When the restaurant check comes at the end of a meal, now it goes to the wife. She reviews it, takes out the credit card or tells him which one to use. After all, he hasn't seen an actual bank statement or bill in years!

When they first started out, he was the alpha dog, grabbing checks whenever they went out, doling money for treats, balancing the budget and dominating the financial planning of their life. Not so much now.

Money streams in from whatever source and finds its way into the household checking account that he is not allowed to see. No one questions it and life is more peaceful that way.

Whether it's a first and only marriage or the last as we near the home stretch, patterns seem to repeat.

In the kitchen, the dinner routine goes from a set time every night to an open ended conversation about restaurants, take-out or grazing. We don't shop for planned meals anymore because if I buy for three evenings a week, we only cook on two, bringing us back to the restaurant game.

Cleaning the house is most aptly represented by that TV commercial where Bernie sees his wife climbing up on ladders and working hard until someone delivers a Swiffer. One of my dear friends once said, "Why doesn't Bernie get off his ass and help her?" which is far more realistic in my view.

Many of us are retired, take up daytime space at home more than ever before and the other is going crazy because they're home together all day and night. The ultimate switch is the final challenge.

We are now cast in opposite roles when the retired spouse still has the working mindset with no place to apply it. He, or she, may supervise and direct the other about things they've never participated in for 40 years!

I have heard discussions about loading dishwashers to grocery shopping that were never a problem until they had to do it together. Some are downright hilarious and I have great empathy for those going through it.

Personally I don't have that particular problem. In our home, he wasn't interested before and he certainly isn't interested now. He's very thankful for what I do, has infinite patience, and is content to wait until it I get around to it.

Somewhere there's a middle ground, but in the meantime, I'm still having a great time and I refuse to take any of it too seriously.

Here we go again!

When I found myself single again, I realized that I wanted to move forward and meet new people. It was a hard decision to make after losing my husband to Covid early on. Of all his health battles, the worst thing happened and there I was alone again.

First you get through the initial shock and then you take inventory of your life. I did that one day at a time but time is not guaranteed. Being a senior changes the expectation. I am much more flawed than I was 20 years ago. Or even 10 years ago. And there are days when I'm pretty drained.

Some are content to live alone and not engage or take chances. I'm not one of those. I'm wired to be social and though I'm not overly adventurous, my mother taught me always to move ahead and live life with optimism.

Being optimistic can be downright hilarious. I chose a senior dating site and told the truth. I'm not so sure all the people who contacted me were truthful and I think a few flunked out of grade school. Others were very specific with what they wanted. Only a manufactured doll could qualify for them, I'm sure.

I had 3 meetings and I ran laughing from 2. The 3rd was too young but really a nice person. I have no idea what anyone thought of me and that's OK. I jumped off and then I got a really awesome message that perked my interest. Intelligent, handsome and a killer smile. So I jumped back on for a day and now we've been dating since last February.

But as we get older, the game changes and so do we. My 9:00 bedtime is challenged on date night so I am not a sparkling joy as the evening wears on. And I can no longer drive safely in the dark so I need a designated driver.

Toby Keith summed it up perfectly when he sang "I'm not as good as I once was, but I'm as good once as I ever was."

Senior dating checklist

Last month I wrote about dating again and all is well in the kingdom. However, what I didn't write about are the little quirky and new things we have to deal with as we get older.

When you live alone, household chores may not be your #1 priority. I do my laundry but I hate fluffing and folding so I take things out of the dryer and they sit on the dining table. It's a new decorator choice. Naturally by the time I get to it, I have to put them back in the dryer to get the new wrinkles out. And the cycle repeats.

Suddenly I'm on a deadline! He's picking me up in 2 days for dinner and I still have to put things away. I need more advance warning.

Cut to the real stuff and there's that sex talk. Do you want it? Can you still do it? How's your arthritis doing? Can you twist and turn? First you act shocked but secretly you're glad someone else brought it up.

Sleep habits are a big one too. If you advance to spending the night together, there are things you want to know. Do you snore? Does he? What do your wear to bed? How many times do you get up to go to the bathroom?

Do you like to sleep with dogs? Do you even like dogs? My sister gave me a mug that says, "Everything tastes better with dog hair in it." Does that include your pillow?

Food is a biggie. All your tastes are pretty well established by now so when the other person pours salt on everything, does it make you crazy? How do you ever cook for them if you don't like salt? Before every meal, don't forget to ask, "Did you take your pills?"

People mention politics and religion often when speaking of compatibility. Interesting banter and differing opinions can be fun if you show mutual respect. Just don't forget to include the little day-to-day habits.

Laugh at your limitations together. I wouldn't have it any other way!

The senior boyfriend

I'm sure if men are reading this, you'll make faces and perhaps be mildly annoyed. Just remember you have gazillions of observations about us so choose your battles wisely.

The senior boyfriend brings some minor challenges that you either accept or reject depending on how the columns add up.

Chances are you've both had full lives before and most of your daily routines are pretty much set. The idea of adjusting to habits, perspectives and annoying quirks has never been a consideration before.

Now he takes over that special chair in the living room, plays with his phone while you're watching TV and hates his hearing aids so the sound is up to levels that break glass. As you adjust and actually get used to it, the dogs hide to get away from the noise.

Bedtime never seems to be in sync but he lays there like a good boy staring at the ceiling while you fall asleep instantly. Then you get up because the dog announces she's ready for breakfast at 7am. He stays in bed. Poor guy didn't get much sleep so you leave him alone. It's a good time to watch your girly shows without hearing big sighs of frustration.

Mealtimes are an enormous challenge. When I'm alone I take some stupid combination of whatever is there and make something out of it. But when he's here, I feel I have to prepare a balanced meal and demonstrate skills as a homemaker. The best way to avoid that is to suggest we go out. That works most of the time.

Let's talk about "droppings" for a bit. Those are clothes, shoes, napkins, gadgets from Amazon and let's not forget papers! There are important papers all over the place but heaven forbid I put them in one place. Organized chaos is his specialty.

Bodily noises come into play at our age. Enough said.

I could go on but everything is new again and I really love it and him. The adjustments are many so we keep laughing and life is good. Humility left the room.

The lighter side of senior sex

As we all have read, a sex life should be enjoyed for as long as you are able. Your endorphins love it and those connections with someone you love makes your life that much better.

However, no one talks about the lack of coordination when you are arthritic or the lack of strength in your knees when required. Kissing and stretching to reach special places creates new challenges too.

Suddenly, in the middle of it all, you hear an "ouch" or a groan and push on anyway so as not to ruin the moment for your partner. Thank goodness the lights are dim and no one can see your face all scrunched up.

Body shaming is a thing of the past so do not worry about that now. The changes that happened over the years lead to directing each other to new places that gravity hit. Things are squishier and flop differently.

Sooner or later you'll have the discussion about what positions actually work. Scissors may be the "go to" and animal poses don't do it anymore. You are permitted animal noises though. The first order of business is to determine if your body will agree to bend.

Talking about it starts off seriously and usually evolves into hysterical laughter. There is no way to be offended because there's no one to blame. Whatever you did or experimented with at 20 or 30 is not going to happen no matter how much ibuprofen you take.

We never explain anything to the kids who are now in their 40's and 50's because they cringe at the thought. You will forever hold the secret of senior gymnastics private.

Sex can be full-on, full-speed ahead or it can be a cuddle fest. It doesn't much matter anymore. We've earned the right to be uncoordinated.

Alexa can give you all the mood music you could ever want and a drink can mellow and relax you, so setting your expectations on just plain enjoying yourselves, and the intimacy of being together, can turn the moment into a party.

Decisions & spats

Once upon a time making simple decisions about hanging a picture or what to make for dinner was easy. Now it's a whole process and takes ten times longer than it used to so by the time I've figured it out, I'm too tired to do it.

Hanging a picture requires a hammer, hook and usually a ladder. Climbing up the ladder is not my best event. In fact I tremble each time I have to change an air filter in the house.

I've learned to put pillows on a desk, table or whatever is nearby so I can get up and kneel on the pillows in the hope of reaching the spot to hammer in the hook. It's very calculated and exhausting so several pictures have been leaning on the floor for about 2 years now.

The dinner question is ridiculous. On workdays, the conversation usually goes from "What do you want for dinner?" to "I'm not hungry because I ate an egg sandwich at 2:00" to "So what should I do?" etc. It's a never ending cycle of nonsense and indecision usually ending at one of three local places. Neither one of us can actually make a choice.

We have little spats about whether to leave the car windows open in the garage or if turning light switches on and off uses more electricity or not.

As for the car windows, we keep the trash bins also in the garage and sometimes they smell at the end of the week. (*A little trick I once learned is to freeze your food garbage until trash day and then forget it's there.*)

Open the car windows and everything stinks on 100+ degree days. Keep them closed and the car is really warm. What to do? He says open and I say close.

To solve the electricity problem, I did my research and unfortunately that answer is more complicated than I anticipated. Is your lighting fluorescent, energy saving or traditional? Some lighting has to warm up and it may not be a savings but overall we should turn them off. I lost that argument in 2017 however years ago I was right. Progress got me again.

So how many times has anyone gone to the back yard and left the door open only to hear "How long do you think it will take to air condition the yard?" I don't know. Shall we put it to the test?

Now we have solar lights on the property and to make them look pretty, you have to pick a spot where the sun will reach them. This spat involves morning sun, afternoon sun or setting sun. And so it goes.

Senior couples therapy

This subject can be very serious but also has its humor as we trudge down the road to life changes, retirement, aging and of course, that pesky little issue of drifting off in thought for no apparent reason.

So you decide to consult with a professional but that seems kind of stupid after all these years. You've both survived kids, money challenges, job shifts, moves and all the changes that happen over a lifetime. What's there to discuss?

As you're both sitting at home watching *Dateline*, he starts playing with his phone. And suddenly the sounds from his chair get louder and there's a jet fighter sailing across the living room! He loves videos of jets.

And let's not forget the phone. Back when we were younger, the most complicated cell phone was a little flip and it took an hour to text anyone because you had to count on numbers to write anything.

Now we have sophisticated computers we wear like leashes and barely understand their functions. At least once a week, someone pushes the wrong button, screws up the phone, shuts down the ringer and the tension begins.

How about shopping? Let's look at the internet bargains we absolutely have to buy from China for 59 cents. How I ever lived without that scrubber is beyond me! And the window scraper? Hot plate stands that fold like umbrellas, 50 tangelos that will be out of season next month and since we have nothing else to do, let's overfeed the dogs.

You can't go ballistic on your partner but as we get older, the urge to scream and yell can get stronger too. Self-control and ignoring all the little new quirks make you either turn into a raving lunatic or you play deaf, dumb and blind. I choose the latter.

Therapy is not happening. Pet the dogs. Buy a stuffed animal if you must. Eat rum raisin ice cream. Figure out that phone and call your BFF to exchange stories. And above all, hide his cell phone if you can get away with it!

Adventures with Food

Defending my right to change the menu

I was reminded the other night I have never ordered dinner in a restaurant without making some kind of change to the menu. At first I denied it but admittedly it's true.

I want to know what's on my plate with as few surprises as possible. From fine dining to the burger stand, no one is exempt.

Order a Greek salad for lunch with grilled chicken and you might get it all chopped up, tossed, over-dressed and soggy, olives with pits, olives without pits and the ultimate garnish that changes the whole taste which was the reason you ordered it in the first place.

My husband doesn't like raw onions. He doesn't like when I eat raw onions for obvious reasons so I have to ask if salads have onions. If they're grilled onions, they don't have the same consequence. Since most salads won't have grilled onions, we're back to changing the menu again. The fried onion strings clustered on the tops of salads are pretty neutral but not good for your health.

I've also learned to ask about lettuce. The spring mix, though attractive on a plate, is really a bag of lawn cuttings. I'm sure there's a landscape van out back making daily deliveries. I want real lettuce or spinach. It can be romaine or iceberg. Please don't give me a pile of green and red leaves with stems.

Moving on to garnish, paprika can taste dreadful but chefs believe it looks pretty so they sprinkle it everywhere. Parsley flakes are a common garnish and get piled up on your plate like a wreath around your entrée. You can't get rid of it.

How about kale? And the other dark, leafy green things placed under your grilled food when served? What do you do with it? It's soggy, tasteless and useless, and I have to find a place to put it so I can eat my dinner.

Side dishes are either lovely mixed medleys of overdone carrots, broccoli and cauliflower or, if you're very lucky, you might get zucchini. The peas and carrots of yesteryear don't come up too often anymore. Asparagus is extra.

Potatoes are baked, mashed, sautéed, real and boxed. French fries can be seasoned, crinkle-cut, fresh-cut, curly, or homemade chips. If you want them plain, no one knows what to do. Anyone remember Bob's Big Boy fries and bleu cheese dressing? The best!

A few questions have backfired on me. I've learned never to ask if potatoes are real or meat is fresh in certain coffee shops. It doesn't go well and my friends can't stop laughing.

My husband jumped on the bandwagon and now, after I've gone through my ordering routine, he will ask for his food to be piled up in the shape of the Empire State building or something equally absurd. It's fun to see how long it takes the server to figure us out.

We're too involved in cooking shows, tastings and presentation. Please give me selections that are easy to understand so I don't get all befuddled and embarrass my husband and friends.

The food has very little to do with the restaurant choice

Eating out is all too common for us because of work schedules and just plain bad habits. We have learned our way around neighborhood eateries and picking favorites has very little to do with food quality.

You would think choosing a place to dine would be based on the menu. Alas, it's not. It's not even about price! Our biggest measurement is about the ambiance, or lack thereof.

At our time of life, walking in to the blaring sound of rap or heavy metal is bad for the digestion.

Remember when your Mom said you would ruin your hearing playing rock-n-roll too loudly? Can you imagine their reactions to the hip-hop, rap, banging and pounding of today's music? Back then, Elvis and the blues were over the top. What would they have done with Miley Cyrus? No one wants to eat with that!

Young people are basically going deaf. Fortunately for them, when they reach our age, it won't matter what anyone plays because they won't hear it anyway.

Let's also mention seating and the distance between the table and the back of the booth. The tables are in fixed positions but the menu is loaded with pasta. Kind of defeats the point of serving high calorie meals if you can't fit into the booth.

As for the tables with chairs, if they're light weight or flimsy, it's hard to stay balanced and women have no place to hang a purse. If you're not carrying around one of those ornamental table hooks, what do you do? I'm not in favor of putting it on the floor with all the French fries from the family before us.

Now they have tabletop computer games and self-serve options. So if I can order and pay myself, all I really need is a busboy to bring the food. I expect one day the food will come around on a conveyer belt and we'll have to grab it as it goes by. (Images of Lucy at the chocolate factory now pop into my head.)

If I want to play games, they charge me extra. I'm not seeing the advantage for the server who counts on tips if we're not even using the dining service they provide. Do we cut their tips? That doesn't seem right.

And, most important is that I always change the menu anyway. Last year I wrote "Defending My Right to Change the Menu" and received emails from readers just as frustrated as me. How do I get what I want from a tabletop computer?

There still are several places around town that actually consider us senior patrons. We can get $10.00 specials in a formal restaurant setting with no noise, good old fashioned fried chicken in another without going to a drive-thru, great breakfast specials in others and hope is not lost.

Sports bars with the sexy girl theme are everywhere and if you can still converse over the 30 TV screens hanging above your head, and get past the music and cheering, the wings are usually great and really bad for you. As for the girls, they're eye candy for the men.

Next we'll take up fusion cooking. Once upon a time they called that a mistake.

All I wanted was a meal deal

It was a typical day; I was typically late and hungry. I saw a sandwich shop and stopped to get a quick meal deal. And that was when I realized there are no quick solutions to anything anymore.

I had to think about which store to go to because no one has the same sizes. If you're not hungry, go to the one with 4″ sizes but the smallest you can get at another is 6″. How about an 8″? They go from 4″ to 12″ in 4″ steps. A local company offers a really awesome one they call small, but it's actually 12″. How much meat is in it depends on which location.

Another consideration would be the burger chains but they all have paper thin burgers with so much mayo, ketchup, mustard, pickles, tomato and lettuce, that the simple burger is a thing of the past. Then you look at the fat count and your chest tightens just thinking it over.

As for chicken and fish chains, the real decision is how much batter you want on it. The chicken and fish are pretty hard to find. I reserve my visits to them on days when I enjoy emotional eating binges.

I have a reference guide in my car.

I picked one of the national chains and watched my sandwich go down the line, added the side and asked to include a drink. So far, so good. I paid with my debit card and then took a couple of minutes to put it away, get my empty cup, grab my bags, look for napkins and saw that the people and other sandwiches were piling up behind me.

That made me rush more and accomplish less. I felt like Lucy on the candy line for those of you who love vintage TV.

Off to the drink machine and it's a damn computer! You have to push something to get the ice and I pulled instead. Then you have to dial up what you want and go through 2 more screens to pick the exact drink but when it's time to push, it's not in the same place.

How do they keep 50 different drinks in there?

A young woman was behind me, one of many by now, and she was kind enough to help me out. I let her go first so I could watch. The line was getting longer and now people were reaching over each other to find cup lids and straws, ready to pounce when I completed my task.

I gathered all the necessary components, balanced them as well as I could and waddled off to my car. Since I really was hungry, I thought I would take a bite before going to work.

I now know that no matter how you plan ahead, any amount of shredded lettuce on your sandwich is destined to fall out where you can't reach it. There's nothing quite like driving with lettuce in the sun smelling up your car.

So much for the quick meal deal.

Food choices now going my way?

I have always moaned & groaned about restaurant choices but recently I've read about so-called healthy selections and the nutrition expert's opinions were vastly different in 2016.

They've been pushing kale on me for a few years now. I hate kale! Now, suddenly, as if an answer to my plea, I read that a spinach salad with cherry tomatoes is better for my mood than kale. I could have told you that.

Thank goodness dark chocolate has stayed on the list of good mood foods. Oh happy day!

I'm still wrestling with the Bloomin' Onion now classified as a mood killer. It never killed my mood although I do have a lot of food guilt when I eat it. But it passes quickly.

And it really is true that as you get older, your food consumption goes down almost in auto mode. So how come the weight doesn't go down with it? You would think that after all these years there would be some kind of reward for eating less. There's something almost sinister in that.

Restaurants still have to decorate and change everything so the new normal is explaining what you don't want as opposed to what you do. To accomplish that, they have to manually take your order and figure out how to translate it into a computer entry for the cooks. Anyone ever think to walk into the kitchen and just tell them?

I was pretty happy to learn about beef & cheddar being better than turkey, ranch and bacon sandwiches. And now avocado is the magic food of the year so guacamole dip is guilt free along with a crab & avocado stack from Marie Callenders. I haven't solved the chips dilemma.

And did you know that a cup of hot & sour soup has 7,980 mg. of sodium? Whoa! That will blow up your blood pressure! Not good for Chinese restaurants. No offense meant.

On the good list are cranberries, red grapes, blueberries, lots of different seafood, and a vast assortment of creations designed to improve your brain, sleep habits, sugar intake, blood pressure and all around health. It doesn't tell you to eat things in any particular order just so long as you spread them out over the day.

It's a little bothersome that I'm finishing up my 60's soon and I have to re-group. I thought I had already re-grouped when I learned about blood pressure, salt and carbs. Guess I went there but didn't do it right.

No one ever explains how long it takes to notice changes so we need to have faith it's a quick fix for a lifetime of food blunders.

Remember the comedy routine about Dad giving kids chocolate cake for breakfast and justifying it? It contained chocolate, eggs, flour and so on. It was just a question of how you assembled it.

Now with chocolate remaining the list, along with other ingredients, I can have chocolate cake and stay within the guidelines, right?

It's actually a wonder we've lasted this long!

The question that never gets answered

What is the one question I ask my husband every single day? It's always the same and the answer is always the same. No matter how prepared I think I am, we go through this over and over and over again. You would think at our age we could get it answered.

"What do you want to do for dinner?"

There are no less than 20 restaurants around us and we know every menu item by heart. Some servers actually know I hate garnish on my food too.

Whether or not we eat at home hardly comes into play with my schedule. I'm never prepared to cook, he doesn't cook and if I buy things to cook, they spoil in the fridge waiting for one of us to do something.

But if I go to the market on the way home to buy something to make, it's too late to cook because the desired eating time passed an hour before I got home. Kind of defeats the whole purpose of being a domestic goddess.

The idea of calling a delivery service is not appealing unless you're stuck home sick and absolutely must have chicken soup from the deli. Anyway, that process takes over 1-2 hours and by then we've landed on the couch for the nightly TV marathon.

My friend suggested living by crock pot. Not happening. After a few of those, they all taste the same and the urge for Mallomars or Baskin-Robbins takes over.

Then there are frozen dinners. So many advertise healthy alternatives and yet, dried up string beans and no-salt saucy chicken in a microwave is good for you because you can't stand to eat it, therefore you involuntarily diet and get healthy. (*Reminds me of "alternative facts" but that's a whole other article.*)

Rummaging around the fridge is that last resort and by that time it's 7:00 or 8:00 and old people don't eat after 6:00PM, or so I'm told. They snack and by definition, a snack has no boundaries or requirements to be anything but tasty. Problem solved.

Back in the restaurants again!

We're headed for the best season of the year with everyone figuring out how to safely go to restaurants and movies. With Thanksgiving this month and Christmas following, all wrapping up with New Year's Eve, we're jazzed and ready to go!

But, and there's always a but, the places now have smaller menus and all the chefs put their spin on everything so they stand out. No one considers that maybe we want to enjoy the classics we were deprived of while on lock-down.

I always fuss about garnish and additives that are not listed on the menu but now I have absolutely no idea what I'm going to get. When I would order a Chicken Piccata, I expected a nice light lemon butter and wine sauce and capers on chicken. I ask for them not to put the garnish on and then this mess shows up at the table.

Salt and seasonings, including little round things (not capers) are in the wrong color thick sauce and it's on a bed of mashed potatoes. The chicken is actually either heavily breaded or it's a quarter-chicken. Please hire an old chef who can cook traditional meals! A little angel hair pasta and extra sauce would be so appreciated.

Now the next day's breakfast presented new problems. Remember corned beef hash from a can, fried and crispy on the outside? Today it's a homemade hash and when it shows up, it's stringy and as if it isn't naturally salty anyway, they add more salt. Back it goes.

Moving on, I ordered a grilled chicken dinner somewhere and it came with a white barbecue sauce over it. At least I was smart enough to ask for it on the side so when it burned my tongue, I didn't have to scrape it too much. However the potato salad with it was very strange. The kitchen unloaded a shaker of some unidentified spice.

Everyone's a chef! When Thanksgiving comes around, I guess they'll serve tofu turkeys like Marie did on *Everyone Loves Raymond* in the 80's. Not for me.

Restaurant music

We go to a lot of restaurants because our days get so hectic that there's no time to cook. We have our favorites of course but nowadays I have to ask if they play music before I actually commit to eating somewhere new.

If you wear hearing aids and try a contemporary place, the chances are they play music from another planet at a level that makes dogs run away. Even without hearing aids, having a conversation without 40 "What?" and 20 "Say that again please" moments is near impossible.

If you ask a young person to turn it down a bit, they never commit. They say they'll ask the manager and by that time you're ready to go. The manager hides a lot.

When you set up a sweet, romantic dinner and they have musicians, you may as well forget the romance. Although it looks great on a movie screen, personally I think having a violin in my face is a bit intrusive and I don't know whether to smile or swat it away like a fly.

Whichever it is, the moment has passed and now there's a big bill at the end. And then you have to be mindful because the musicians are entitled to be tipped.

Is there any way to call a place and ask what their music is? What's the volume level? Are there quiet corners where people can dine and hear themselves think?

Remember the days of boom boxes and transistor radios? What if I brought one into a restaurant and simply explained that they can turn off their music because I brought my own? I would love to see how that gets handled. Then I would turn on the 50's station and rock the twist with Chubby Checker.

I haven't figured this out yet so the pressure is on. I'm not planning on improving my domestic skills anytime soon so I am developing a list of places to go that meet my criteria. Soft music, adequate lighting, simple food with no creativity and comfortable booths.

I'll let you know.

Broccoli

Do you remember your parents telling you that there would be no dessert if you didn't eat your vegetables? Did you push them under the mashed potatoes or maybe the pieces floated off your plate on their own and into the dog's mouth?

We all had little tricks to get around dinner rules. And now, when I'm regressing in my golden years, I cook things because I'm supposed to. I don't actually like it and I'm sucked back into that mindset of getting away with pushing my veggies around the plate to try and make them look smaller.

I have this vision in my head of my mother gently explaining how important my vegetables are and trying to reason with me. I also remember the words "your thumb is not a pusher" when I can't always get everything on my fork. I know she's up there!

Let's take a look at broccoli: It's a pretty little veggie and looks great in photos. In fact, it's so distinctive that there's a tree in the Vatican they call a broccoli tree because it looks like a giant piece of broccoli. And yes, it's true.

Who likes broccoli? We know that President Bush (the 1st one) hated it. Maybe it was banned in the White House?

We also know that most restaurants don't offer it as part of your dinner when they can use overcooked mushy mixes instead. If you want broccoli, you pay an up-charge.

Personally I have gone from hating it to loving it and back to hating it again. My guy loves it and drowns it in red wine vinegar so I make sure to have Italian dressing on my salad when he eats broccoli so my nose doesn't get confused.

Cooking broccoli is an art. You put it in the steamer but timing it out isn't easy. If it's just a small amount, adjusting the timer is tricky. I wind up checking it every 5 minutes to make sure the color looks right.

So I stick with easy stuff now. Peas, string beans, spinach and a few others.

It's Holiday Time

A valentine to the House Royalty

I've been reminded recently that I have nothing to do with how the household runs and neither does my husband. In fact, no humans are involved.

The interactions between us are overshadowed by rules set down by 2 spoiled Shih Tzu's and the most lovable old Golden Retriever on the planet. The golden just goes along with everything because that's his nature. I can learn some lessons from him.

With rubber-backed rugs all over for our old boy, and beds of soft microfiber and fluffy stuff, we step over everything and have only one route to the couch.

On holidays we add the leaves to the table and things get re-arranged much to the dismay of these kids who now have to find new ways to show they're in charge. They don't want to miss anything so lying down in everyone's path seems to work and they gain 5 pounds when we have guests.

Bedtime is ridiculous. Yes, they know the routine but every year they get closer to pushing us out of bed. They lie down between us, sideways of course, and have to stretch out as much as possible 4 or 5 times before settling down.

And my pillow has become a throne for the commander of this group. I actually have slept on a corner of the pillow so as not to disturb him. The Golden is perfect and just lies alongside the bed.

If we want them to stay off the bed for a little while, one goes to the far end and curls up in a little ball and the other throws a fit, moans, drags pillows around and generally makes sure we know he's mad. The Golden just continues to be perfect.

We watch the dog shows on TV and know we're supposed to show leadership. But these guys are amazingly well behaved in every way as long as no one interferes with their routines.

Daylight savings really messes with us. The sun goes down early and they start dancing around for their supper. It's almost ritualistic! If we tell them it's only 4pm, they don't care. So for an hour we have eyes drilling holes in us watching for any signs of movement.

To all you dog servants out there, know you are automatically elevated to a perfect person. A dog only asks of you what he gives and that's love and loyalty. Too bad they don't cook too but you can't have everything.

This Valentine's Day I thank the puppies for reminding me to be kinder and smile more. On my worst days they look at me with those huge eyes and I am pure mush.

Use the good dishes on Father's Day

When we moved in 2010, I packed all the collectibles, good china, serving pieces, linen napkins and special memorabilia carefully between layers of foam and bubble wrap. The cartons have huge red letters spelling out "fragile" or "this side up" all over them.

I didn't even trust the movers to load them on the truck. The boxes were gently put in my vehicle because I'm the only one who could be trusted to drive with them. I'm happy to say everything made it safely.

It took about 6 months to unpack the everyday stuff and then I needed another few months to relax and enjoy being somewhat settled. No rush.

Now it's been 3 years. I have apologized to guests for serving informally when the occasion called for formal. I cannot even recall how many times I thought up excuses for not using real linen when a dressed table would have been perfect.

Our family was not formal; however, my parents understood and celebrated certain events with style and my father's ever-so-present elegance. They opened the leaves of the living room table and set up for company, holidays, birthdays and anniversaries.

Daddy was a scholar and the most gentle man I've ever known. He was a Professor and loved to teach. He wasn't big on the administrative side of universities so he resigned as head of his department to spend more time in the classrooms and lecture halls.

He was mugged in the streets twice near Columbia University in New York City and even then, he continued to go to the 3 universities he was affiliated with every day. On off days he was at the main New York City Library on 5th Avenue & 42nd Street doing research.

My father wore 3-piece suits and his shirts were always crisp and clean even after he wore them. Sorting laundry was a challenge since you could never tell the dirty shirts from the clean ones unless he showed you.

Back to the dishes. My first real memory of their significance was my parent's 25th anniversary party. Everything was shiny and beautiful. The silver was polished, serving dishes filled with steamy, tasty choices and I was told not to stick my fingers into anything.

I was allowed to eat on those dishes any time they were used. My parents never sent me to the kitchen. I learned my table manners with those dishes but I must confess I still hear my mother say "Your thumb is not a pusher!" It's still hard not to use my thumb.

Recently I've been thinking a lot about those dishes. I think it's time to use them. They are part of our family going back to my grandparents in the late 1800's.

Hey Santa, I'm over here!

So now we're all grown up and live in the real world. Imaginary fairies and elves don't peer from behind doorways or fly overhead. Or do they?

As I get older, I see things changed around in my house all the time. I know I had nothing to do with it. The dogs are too short to do table arrangements but somehow all these festive things start showing up around the end of October. It's really very nice.

I realize as I clean the closets and continue to sort out 50 years of stuff, everything is new again. Putting out figurines, doilies, hand-made wreaths, ornaments, turkeys, etc. brings up all sorts of feelings from holidays past. I look at them all differently now and smile a lot.

At dusk, it's easy to see images of the kids when they were young peeking around the corner. Even the dog sleeping next to my feet is outlined before me. And the train set that circled the tree still trips me up in my imagination even though I don't set it out these days.

Certain ornaments are keepsakes and others are fashion statements. The years when you decorated in monotones were a real challenge. The years of plaids and wood made everyone seem "a little bit country." We had holidays in marshmallow colored bows and icicles, others in bright red and a few very traditional years of popcorn strings.

We stopped using glass ornaments because they are in direct conflict with the dogs. Shiny, light-catching objects that break are just too tempting.

Whatever your faith, there's bound to be a holiday tradition in there somewhere between Halloween and New Year's Eve. Notably it will also involve a candle.

Candles are great little additions to the spirit of any season. They provide dim, romantic light, good smells, work well in the guest bathroom and make your living room smell like an apple pie every day! By January, you don't care if you ever see or smell an apple pie for at least another year.

Now I'm living in an age-restricted community and the kids are parents with children of their own. They are creating their own traditions and we are guests. The role play switch is here. We show up bearing gifts, offer to help with the dishes and secretly hope they'll tell us to sit down and enjoy the day.

We also bring our special holiday dish to the house, try not to get our feathers ruffled when another guest brings the same thing and all around, there's a joy and sadness that the chaos is in someone else's home.

So Santa, when you're on your rounds, don't forget the empty-nesters who championed for you and brought a little magic to the party. Some of us don't travel much anymore. We still have decorations in the house and a little something is always a joy. Whatever way you celebrate, pass the word.

With a little sadness for holidays gone by and lost loved ones, I'm also filled with appreciation for the spirit of giving and sharing as always. Treasure the moments and make new memories!

Changing tradition?

It's that time again! I love fall and all the fun stuff we get to do when it's not blazing outside. We sit in the yard after dinner; we walk dogs without having to put booties on their paws and can finally remember why we waited out the summer. Best of all, the power bill goes down.

Even the mailbox key doesn't stick in the cooler weather. Things just get better all around.

So now it's time to prepare for those Norman Rockwell moments when we celebrate the holidays with traditional family bonding dinners. There are movies made about all the chaos and conflicts but they usually end with the entire group sitting down in a Connecticut dining room that seats 18 all toasting each other.

Thanksgiving calls for turkey, ham, sweet potatoes, pies, stuffing, mashed potatoes (you can never have too many potatoes) and whatever family recipe has been passed through generations for more food than any average human can consume.

Thanksgiving is on a Thursday so we can be sure to have leftovers for the entire weekend because no one can move for about 3 days anyway.

This is by far my favorite holiday but for a different reason than most. I was actually adopted and brought home to my parents just before Thanksgiving. It became my special time and I can be very territorial about it. Nobody messes with my Thanksgiving!

Lately I've been thinking I should change it up. I've seen some really funny reruns of "Everyone Loves Raymond" where Debra serves fish but sure enough, Marie shows up with a turkey anyway. And then on the soap opera "General Hospital" they always have a disaster on Thanksgiving and wind up eating pizza.

(And yes, I have watched that soap since the 60's and I can count on it when life changes the cast of my own life.)

For years when I was in the television industry, we used to have huge dinners because so many actors were away from home working on shows. They may have been shooting the next day so we had the holiday at our house with up to 30 or 40 people I barely knew.

Now I have a small house, and many loved ones are gone so I have the perfect opportunity to scale things down. Yet last year we managed to have 10 for dinner, sent food for another 6 to a friend's home and followed the standard menu choices.

I think the lesson of the day is that no matter how much I would like to do something quirky or change it up, I cannot mess with tradition. I imagine we'll do it again this year.

Retro Christmas list

What if you made a list of all your favorite things from past Christmas holidays and left it on the table for Santa. What would be on it?

I didn't have a Barbie. I had a Revlon doll with blonde hair. She was my friend and lived in an apartment building that was the bookcase in my room. It was hard to find clothes for her so I had to ask Santa. After all, he could find everything!

Pez dispensers and candy! Need I say more?

Of course, where there's candy, there are little pellets that would snap in your mouth and although I can picture the bag, I have no idea what they were called. They were the real snap, crackle & pop of treats.

We didn't ask for expensive computers or cell phones. But I was out-of-my-mind happy when I got a pink princess phone. OMG it even lit up the dial at night! Wow! I could stuff it under my covers and have conversations late at night and no one would know. Or so I thought.

Then I got a real hair dryer once. The kind that had a cap that would blow up with hot air from a big tube attached. I would have to sit under it for about an hour with these huge rollers but it was worth it. I felt so grown up.

And speaking of grown up, when I transitioned from socks to stockings, I could dress up on holidays with new shoes and wear them. Back then they had seams and you had to wear garters. I didn't mind.

I got a brownie camera too. It took great pictures for its time and I still have them. I found some of the negatives in a box so maybe I'll give myself a present and have them digitized.

I wanted a cat. I already had a bird. That cat was awesome and liked to sneak out the window of our 8th floor NYC apartment to walk on the ledge. Surprisingly though, nothing ever happened to him. He would just come in the other window until we figured it out and blocked him. I think he gave us dirty looks but who can tell with a cat?

There were always the familiar pajamas, sweaters, gloves and scarves but when I got the saddle shoes, I knew I had hit the jackpot! So you can only imagine a few years later what the penny loafers meant. I found the shiniest matching pennies and inserted them in the slots of my sable leather shoes with pride. It was a defining moment and I was part of the "in" crowd.

Yay! It's Christmas!

Gifts for a maturing woman

December is the month of giving but I find that as I age, I get gifts all year long without even asking!

Benefits of getting a little older include hair changes. I may not have to shave my legs as often but I have new places to pluck. And the hair on my head experiences major color changes all on its own. Instead of a smooth transition to silver, it gets a skunk-like pattern as it grows.

Wearing make-up is problematic too. It is meant to enhance your features but if you have prominent laugh lines or birds feet, it settles into the worst parts of your face and you are a wicked witch. No make-up at all isn't always a great solution either.

The permanent make-up tattoo thing is terrific actually. What turned me on to it was how so many older women's eyes look kind of hollow and just a little touch of shade between the lashes changes all that. I hated doing it but I loved the result.

Now the spidery veins start showing on top of your hands and sometimes your forearms. If your hands are in a downward position, they pop up all over the place. The only way to hide it is to keep them elevated so the blood flows down and they collapse. It's hard to eat that way.

And how about that crepe paper leg stuff? The shape is still OK but my old beach days have caught up with me big time! No amount of Gold Bond will smooth that out anymore.

So let's talk about skin tone. I always had a smooth olive complexion that now has designs all over it. They're just random spots with no particular pattern and freckles! I never had freckles before and I can't figure out how to give them back. I've been checked over carefully and nothing is suspicious, just not very flattering.

I have now received my gifts for the holidays and all I need is a very glittery outfit to go with them. HAPPY HOLIDAYS TO ALL!

Where's the Easter Bunny?

I want my Easter basket! Thanksgiving, Christmas and Valentine's Day all came and went without parties, dinners or watching everyone open gifts. The living room should have cluttered with torn wrapping paper at Christmas, tons of leftovers on Thanksgiving for turkey sandwiches & football and flowers with chocolate on Valentine's Day.

So now it's time for chocolate bunnies and marshmallow eggs. I think diabetics should get a pass on holidays especially when we have 3 to make up for this year.

Las Vegas casinos give you gifts on holidays. One year they gave us an Easter bunny stuffed toy, He's very cute but acquired the nickname "Stoner Bunny" because he either got loaded on chocolate or smoked something.

But I know where the Easter bunny is! He is in my yard looking sadly at my dead plants from this winter. He has nothing to chew or tear apart and even the coyotes aren't visiting me.

I wanted to know the origin of the Easter bunny and apparently it is "clouded in mystery" according to what I read. It is not mentioned in any scripture but one thought is the symbol of the rabbit stems from pagan tradition as a goddess of fertility.

It is noted that the Easter bunny first came here in the 1700's from German immigrants in Pennsylvania. The children made nests in which bunnies could lay their colored eggs. Children would also leave carrots in case they got hungry.

Eggs for Easter also represent new life and the tradition of decorating them goes as far back as the 13th century. In Russian high society, people exchanged ornate and sometimes jeweled eggs.

So as we mark a full year of restrictions and for some great sadness, we can see the light shining a bit brighter, visit grandchildren and hide eggs for them to find as tradition takes center stage once again.

I'm beginning to see the quail scurrying about and some birds nesting at least. When summer comes, I will be no doubt complaining about that but for now the idea of spring brings hope after a long winter.

Electronic wishes & other annoying holiday treats

A while back I expressed myself about technology taking the personal touch out of the traditions we held dear such as hand written holiday cards. I refused then, and I refuse now, to use the internet to send a friend a holiday greeting.

Whatever holiday you celebrate, it's supposed to be a time of peace, love and friendship. That actually requires a little effort! To use the internet to avoid a note, a card or a photo is just plain lazy.

As for gifts, they're on line too. We can't fight it. I reluctantly accept that option because going to some of these stores really is a pain anyway. Maybe I'm a hypocrite after all.

So I am still sending cards and notes. And when I look in the mailbox to see someone sent one back, I get so excited! If the annual holiday letter is included, I read every word even if it's boring. Someone actually put thought into the letter and that's wonderful.

Let's move on to re-gifting. That is certainly a slippery slope because my circle of friends is much smaller than it used to be. With friends leaving town and others have passed, many friends know each other so a re-gift is out of the question.

I'm not willing to chance someone going to visit a mutual friend and finding their gift to me sitting on the coffee table. It limits the possibilities so if Pier One doesn't have what I want, I hit the internet.

Now let's talk about all the shopping confusion like Black Friday starting after Halloween or Cyber Monday after Black Friday which now runs through the day after Thanksgiving. The stores don't want you to be with family on Thanksgiving because they're announcing the Black Friday door busters after you've stuffed yourself with turkey and waddled to the store.

And if you happen to survive the layaway counter at Walmart, which starts during the summer, they've killed your spirit entirely so you don't care anymore.

When I was a kid, the holidays were exciting. Everything sparkled, people were happy and Santa was at Macy's on 34th Street. All the stores had glorious moving displays & ice skaters were at

Rockefeller Center or Wolman rink in Central Park. Even subway cars had happy people with shopping bags of gifts. (*Obviously I'm from New York City.*)

Not one person knew what the internet was or how to send an electronic greeting card. We even had a party line phone and it was the one time we would actually butt in to a conversation to send good wishes.

I don't want to return to the 50's but a little less technology and a lot more personal interaction would sure be nice. Happy Holidays to all!

Trivia fun!

Let's just be silly and enjoy some trivia for a change. As we go into the holiday season, we all need a little distraction from the realities of the world these days.

My friend Diana looks up everything! She sends me stuff and ideas all the time. Since it's Thanksgiving and I can't think of anything about turkeys, here we go:

"Over a Barrel" comes from the days before CPR. A drowning victim would be placed over a barrel and rolled back and forth in an effort to empty the lungs of water. It rarely worked so if you are "over a barrel," you are in deep trouble.

"Barge In" refers to freight being moved along on barges along the Mississippi pushed by steamboats. Since they were hard to control, they often would swing into piers or other boats and the expression "barged in" was born.

No piece of paper can be folded in half more than 7 times. Go ahead. We can wait.

The King of Hearts is the only king without a mustache.

American Airlines saved $40,000 in 1987 by eliminating one olive from each salad served in first class. (Really???)

Walt Disney was afraid of mice!

A duck's quack doesn't echo. No one knows why.

"A Shot of Whiskey" cost the same as a .45 cartridge for a six-gun. So if a cowboy was low on cash, he would give the bartender a cartridge in exchange for a drink, hence a "shot" of whiskey.

"Riff Raff" refers to the travel from north to south on the Mississippi where travel on the riverboats was too expensive so many traveled on rafts. They were considered cheap and everything else had the right of way. The steering oar was called a "riff" and this became "riff-raff" implying low class.

So now I have spent time folding paper in half, pricing olives, pulling out decks of cards and asking Alexa to quack like a duck. It is much better than watching the news and I'm good with that.

Hug your loved ones, celebrate life and Happy Thanksgiving to all!

This & That

Random thoughts

The inspiration for this column surfaced when, at 60, I found my life taking unexpected turns and my perceptions of life's ordinary events had vastly changed.

I remember things differently now. For example, every time there's a new, clever and seemingly simple idea advertised on TV, I ask myself "Why didn't I think of that?" Now I consider that perhaps I did think of it and didn't remember. Oddly it makes me feel better.

An editor once told me the basic rules of writing and conversation are the who, what, where, why and when of any story. It gets frustrating now when all that information doesn't show up in my head at the same time.

I also have mixed feelings about potato chip bags. I can't buy chips with a sandwich because I can't open the bag unless I have a scissor. And those little peanut packs on airplanes? OMG! Duck when they pass them out! At least one out of two will send nuts flying through the air when the vacuum seal breaks. Considering our mindset on planes, airlines should reconsider snacks so it doesn't lead to chaos.

Some assembly required doesn't mean what it used to. That's self-explanatory.

I am not a fan of tattoos or body art although I do admit considering something small placed indiscreetly. At my age, it probably won't make much difference and an ankle or shoulder won't sag too much. Imagine years from now how all these 30 and 40-something people with massive body art will look? What used to be reserved for bikers is now a fashion statement. How fashionable will it be when they all sport droopy dragons and skulls?

Have you ever noticed that young people smiling and talking show their upper teeth and older people show their lower teeth. I didn't think much of it at first and then I looked in the mirror. My face dropped and my teeth didn't. And the lower teeth are the ones that move and look like crooked building blocks.

It always takes about 4 people to finish a story. No one in my group can remember all the details so you hear "What was that?" "Where was that?" and "Who was that?" a lot. As if that wasn't frustrating enough, no one can be patient and wait to hear the end of the story that now went into overtime.

We love dogs. The older we get, the smaller our dogs are. I still have my giant sized dog but now we also have a 13 pound Shih Tzu who rules. We call ourselves Mommy and Daddy and act stupid because they're so cute. I guess I should be embarrassed but I'm not.

Thank you for reading. I have now cleared some brain clutter and I'm ready for something new.

Under the desk pad

As the year comes to an end, I find accumulated little scraps of paper with memorable quotes, advice, fortunes, etc. Most are protected under my desk pad, some are fridge magnets and others remain in folders for later. So far I haven't found much use for any of them so sharing here gives them a new purpose.

My annual dog calendar has great quotes such as:

"Dogs feel very strongly that they should always go with you in your car, in case the need should arise for them to bark violently at nothing right in your ear." Dave Barry

"Don't accept your dog's admiration as conclusive evidence that you are wonderful." Ann Landers

How about those fortune cookies? If only we could count on them! I've been told I will inherit a large sum of money from an unusual source. That must be right so if I do inherit something, it will certainly be unusual.

Another cookie asked the question "How can you have a beautiful ending without making beautiful mistakes?" If that's true, I have a whopper of an ending ahead of me for sure.

The refrigerator holds warnings on magnets such as "Be nice to me! With a minimum of effort I can make things very difficult." and "If you can't be a good example, you'll just have to be an excellent warning." Words to live by.

The wishful thinking magnet says "I'm over-pampered and spoiled rotten. I deserve much better than this."

For those days when nothing goes right, we have "Caution. I go from 0 to bitch in 2.5 seconds."

The folder quotes go way back over 30 years from places I've worked. Remember this? "Some things are like Slinkys.....not really good for anything but it still brings a smile to your face when you push it down a flight of stairs."

The definition of stress never changes either. "Stress: Strain, pressure and the internal confusion generated when the mind attempts to override the body's basic urge to choke the living daylights out of some jerk who desperately needs it."

Since this column is about being in my 60's, here's one that came true. From Maxine: "It's scary when you start making the same noises as your coffeemaker!"

A plaque in my kitchen reads "The best antiques are old friends."

I make it a point to regularly comb through things and always get lost in remembering why I saved them. It's entertaining and makes me happy.

With the digital age upon us, I still post what I like all over the place and smile every time I pass by the clutter on my fridge or desk. There's so much that I have to rotate them every few years.

Maybe one day I'll take everything and make a photo book out of it for the coffee table. That may be the only way to sort 40 years of clippings.

And the final words of wisdom from a cookie: "Half of being smart is knowing what you're dumb about." That can keep you busy for a long time.

"Joe sent me"

How many passwords can you remember? I started a list the other day in case of emergency and when I got to 37 combinations, I thought I would hyperventilate so I sat down and petted the dog.

All the news, magazines and digital media tell us to guard our passwords, change them often and worst of all, never use the same one twice. Really?

That is just not possible. I've tried to think of a formula so I would have a hint for each site. I've gone upper case, lower case, numbers in the middle, favorite days, backwards spelling and derivatives from familiar things.

Fraud articles are everywhere. And, as if the password thing isn't enough, according to the AARP Bulletin April 2014, we should visit a site to locate 40 more reports containing our personal information and monitor those also.

Another article says you shouldn't use snail mail because it too is an invitation for identity theft. So exactly what am I supposed to do?

If you run your annual credit report, check the 40 other reports we're told are available, pay bills on line, bank on line, order on line, sell on line and even do work on line, it can add up to a whole lot of access and more than 100 passwords.

Simply put, that's not going to happen in my brain.

During the age of simplicity, I sent a check through the mail and paid my bills. Nothing bad ever happened. Social security numbers were shared and in fact used on return addresses of people in the military.

The first credit card I had was called a Uni-Card and I actually had a job there filing applications that came in the mail. There were no security scanners or armed identity investigators watching me.

Nothing was particularly organized and people weren't suspicious. Credit cards didn't have passwords so the biggest thing to remember was where you put it. Once it was in your hot hand, you could actually use it without 20 questions popping up on a desktop screen they hadn't invented yet.

Now you scan a check so the image goes floating around in

outer space eventually winding up a deposit in your bank account. That just seems wrong!

Our acceptable standards have changed. Big banks and corporations determined that paying out fraudulent checks is cheaper than installing systems to spot the forgeries before anything is transacted. Now there's a policy crafted by geniuses!

There's much talk about the age of technology, children that don't know what hopscotch is and the loss of personalization. And yet we follow like lemmings into the black abyss of computers hoping life as a Jetson will prove as much fun as it appeared when premiered in 1962.

I am pulling back more and more. We were not meant to swim around in all this electronic clutter. My cell phone will never see mobile banking or Facebook or Twitter and Insta-Gram.

My goal is to have less than 5 passwords so I have a better chance at a peaceful life.

What are ides?

Ever since I can remember, the phrase "Beware the ides of March" was just something I heard but had no idea what it meant. So I looked it up.

"Ides of March, a day on the Roman calendar that corresponds to 15 March; it was marked by several religious observances and became notorious as the date of the assassination of Julius Caesar in 44 BC." Wikipedia.

Additionally Wikipedia says that "Ides" marked the approximate middle of the month and for March, May, July and October, it is the 15th and for other months it is the 13th according to Dictionary.com.

There are songs about "St. Ides of March" and even a malt liquor St. Ides named after the Irish saint. Apparently the liquor inspired the songs but who am I to judge?

Now if you go further into this, when used as an acronym, IDES can be Intrusion Detection Expert System and Internet Demonstration and Evaluation System among others.

There is a reference to "IDE" and the word "disambiguation" pops up. Big word for a singular ide. Make one little letter change to "Idis" and you have a being in Germanic paganism. Time to stop.

The phrase itself "Beware the ides of March" is from Shakespeare's "Julius Caesar" written in 1599 and spoken as a warning that his life was in danger. Before then, the "Ides of March" didn't carry with it any sense of dread whatsoever and was considered just another term used in the Roman calendar.

There were 3 specifically named days each month but the exact dates were tied to the moon: They were the Kalends, the first day of the month, the Nones, the 5th or 7th day of the month and the Ides, the middle of the month which usually fell between the 13th and 15th.

It's really very interesting how complicated it was to set an appointment on the Kalends when you didn't know where the moon was or how many days to count. It must have been a real struggle in February.

Translating all this to 2016, we now should be saying "Beware the ides of April" since the taxes are due. Maybe the ides of any month you have a house payment applies also. Go past the ides and there's a late charge.

On the Kalends, I start adding up all my bills and hope that when the Nones comes around I have a pretty good handle on the month's budget.

Can you imagine speaking to anyone in these terms? If it isn't on the phone, they're clueless. Admittedly I had to look all this up because I forget stuff and frankly didn't even recall if I ever knew it in the first place.

At least now if someone refers to the ides of March, I will be able to answer with some certainty and confuse everyone. I can astound my friends with a history lesson and write notes in code. I can date documents with words instead of numbers too.

Just to be on the safe side, I will try my best not to annoy too many people on the 15th just in case.

The evolution of home ownership

In younger days we could fix anything, do anything and modify anything to make it work. From mowing the lawns (and yes, we had lawns back then) to putting handles on cabinet doors or painting the house, we had our respective roles in the home.

There were specific things we trusted the other to do. He did the outside and garage. I did the inside. I made all interior decorating decisions and he made all the outside things look great. I had to give up the pool design since it was outside but that was the deal.

Then his knees went out and so did the lawn. If you can't push the lawnmower, you shouldn't have a lawn. In my case, I had gone wallpaper crazy when bright, bold Waverly patterns adorned the house. To remove it required steamers, scrapers and other tools that my arms just couldn't manage.

So we moved and got into the paint thing, desert landscaping and built-in garage with air conditioning. Such becomes the evolution of home ownership.

But every home requires repairs and a host of honey-do lists weekly. And let's not forget the cars! Change the oil, wash the car yourself so the brushes don't scratch the paint, and so on.

Fast forward and I don't give a thought to the car paint or the ugly rocks in my front yard. Scraping the barbeque is the last thing I want to do so I'm headed out for a new one. And so we reach another moment of change when smaller is better.

I have evolved and now my version of a tiny house is upon us. From what was once a total of 4 homes filled with stuff, we are now in the overwhelming job of downsizing to one small home with barely enough room to turn around.

Headed for that final stage of fixed income, the ultimate goal is keep everything stable for a long time to come. Money drives every decision and our thought processes are permanently altered.

Home ownership is a funny thing. It can be a mark of achievement or an emotional leash creating unwanted stress. The housing crash taught us to let go as we watched all that equity and security vanish.

For those whose homes were all paid for, they just stayed put.

But for us, the old house payment or a reverse mortgage became out of reach. Planning for our future isn't about the equity, it's about the manageability of a lifetime payment.

I write this because I'm pretty sure we're not alone with this challenge. And to those who kick themselves and wonder what they could have done to be free of house payments, don't beat yourself up. So many who did everything right are in the same boat losing pensions and investments once considered conservative and safe.

We're still feeling it and we have to adjust whether we like it or not. As cliché as it is, it is what it is!

Flying pigs are a great idea

Have you ever had an idea, thought it would revolutionize something but when you mentioned it to a friend, they said you were crazy? "That is silly" or "Where are you going to make it?" or how about "How can you protect anything like that?" runs over and over so you drop it entirely.

We watch Shark Tank on TV and admittedly there are some winners and some real losers. In fact, I have a hard time understanding how anyone makes real money on the internet because everything seems too elusive to me.

One friend had a really good idea that got stolen and now she has no money to fight a big company for making her protected product. Not a very nice sandbox to be playing in.

So here they come on TV and either they want to be turned down but get the instant recognition from the show or they sincerely want to have investors and guidance. And I watch, wishing this had been around when I was younger, had the energy, drive and ambition it takes to be an entrepreneur.

About 20 years ago, while on vacation with friends, I brought up cameras on cars. I had seen so many people back up on toys, ongoing traffic and everything in between so it just seemed logical that putting some kind of a camera on the back of a car would work. After all, motor-homes already had them.

You know that hand gesture people make when they think you're not being practical? Wave the hand in front of you and move on! Yup, that's the one and I was waved on.

Then there was the tool to get every bit of product out of a jar. Some person goes on Shark Tank and now makes tons of money selling one with some silly name. I was attaching pieces of sponges to sticks long ago!

No one has figured out how to get a pump bottle to actually pump out all the product inside. I'm hoping that one comes around soon. I'm also hoping for the lip gloss wand to actually reach in to the bottom of the tube.

Another guy takes a piece of plastic (or something like that) and makes a flat pocket out of it to wedge between your car seat and the console. He's making a fortune catching potato chips, crumbs and coins in cars! It actually has an infomercial so if you order, you get 2 for the price of one plus shipping and handling. It costs 25 cents plus probably $1 postage and they're hauling in $20 per order.

I hold a copyright on a game we invented back in the 80's which evolved over a discussion about shipping orders. My assistant said a customer called about their order and I was irritable so I said "Tell them their order will ship when pigs fly." So a board game was born. It's called "Next Day Pig" and everyone has to ship by flying pig and get through the hazards of misdirected flights, weather, broken boxes....well, you get the idea.

Maybe I should give it a try? First I have to get an investor or go on TV. If you see flying pigs, you'll know I finally did it!

Is that music?

My parents came from backgrounds in classical music and opera. I was never a fan of opera. No way to be kind about it. It bored me crazy when my father sat at the kitchen table, cranked up the Zenith needle dial radio and listened to Milton Cross and the Metropolitan Opera every Saturday morning.

But Saturdays were to be spent with my father and every week he took me someplace special in the afternoon. Usually we went to the movies, Radio City Music Hall, a museum or out to lunch. While my mother taught piano every Saturday, my days with Daddy were special.

My parents were sometimes considered intellectual snobs, or so it seemed as a child, and the oncoming new music and trends were quite a contrast to their interests. Mind you, they were far from prudish. They were very progressive thinkers but my Dad's parents were opera performers and music appreciation never included the likes of rock & roll.

Entering my early double-digit years meant American Bandstand rating the beat and taking swing dancing to a whole new place. Yahoo! Saddle shoes were still in but poodle skirts had already passed. Soap operas were fun too and so I developed teen tastes of the time.

There was "a whole lotta shakin' going on" all the way to the peppermint twist, Bobby Rydell, Frankie & Annette singing about the beach and the ultimate of all ultimates, Elvis. Very little made sense to anyone's parents.

Ed Sullivan was only showing the upper half of Elvis because of censors. Even Lucy & Ricky had to sleep in separate beds. Oh, the shame of it all!

Now we're in a new century with new music. I think it's music. They tell me it's music.

Every station on the radio screams noise to me and if a rap song comes on, I cannot understand even one word! The loud banging makes heavy metal of 20 years ago sound classical.

What happened? Since when did expressing yourself to the world through the arts become so violent? You never hear of an old fashioned country singer being murdered but we have news stories about rappers murders often.

The music culture of today needs to make another swing back to calmer, soothing tones. We are craving the harmonies of Earth, Wind & Fire, the amazing creativity of Kenny Loggins, Barry Manilow, The Beatles and Frank Sinatra's music arranged by Nelson Riddle.

It's not about reviving the old; it's about writing music that flows through your brain with some sense of continuity. The banging and fierceness of today's noise is upsetting and actually makes you nervously jumpy when you listen.

The world is ever changing so the inevitability of new noise we don't understand is actually understandable. But whatever that sound of the future may be, I really pray it sends a message of calm and slower rhythms so the banging will stop.

My stepdaughters used to call my music "Mom Rock." I hope it comes back soon.

The guilt stays with you!

Do you tear off the tags on furniture and pillows? How about the magazine inserts that make it impossible to keep the page turned to what you are reading?

Do you ever go in the "out" door at a supermarket? Do you take your empty cart to the rack in the parking lot? Or do you carefully balance it against the cement strip? Maybe you put the front wheels in the planter?

What if the dry cleaner notices your bedspread is tag-less? Will they report you?

I have actually kept the tags on pillows and carefully placed them on the furniture tucked under so nobody can see.

As a child I believed in the tag police. Why not? I also thought there was a tooth fairy so it wasn't a big leap. If the tag was still on the pillow, the tooth fairy would know I deserved a quarter.

Going in the wrong door makes me look dumb so I may bend down and grab one of those magazines they leave for you and pretend I did it on purpose. I remember the old George Carlin routine when the cat accidentally slammed into a glass door, shook himself off and meowed "I meant to do that!"

Who raises their feet off the car floor when going over railroad tracks? Can't take a chance on that bad luck. After all, I don't want to be responsible for everyone in the car if I don't.

Then there's the food shopping guilt that starts at childhood and replays in your head with every trip to the market. "You must eat a balanced diet" and "Don't buy junk food. "Eat nutritious food that puts fuel in the furnace."

And all of a sudden, Hostess offers orange or chocolate cupcakes with icing swirls for $1.00 per package. What's a girl to do? Memories of spending my 25 cents a day after school on cupcakes and Devil Dogs come flooding back. The food is junk in its purest form. Guilt and sugar spikes are forgotten.

My husband has his little quirky things too. He keeps every shipping carton for everything he ever bought Or at least he tries. What if we have to return it?

Empty boxes are like wire hangers. All I want to do is throw them away. Now I understand how Joan Crawford felt.

Every few months I go weave my way through the garage, break them down and create a box sculpture for the recycler. I have to do it when he isn't looking. Inevitably, the one box we will need will be gone and I'll have to take the fall. Nobody wins.

All those little rules that we learned as children are permanently planted in my head. The tags, follow directions, and the ultimate dinner rule for the peas on the plate "Your thumb is not a pusher."

We live with the bells going off in our heads wandering through our daily routines. There's no getting away from it!

Feeling inspired (sort of)

Back in the good old 60's age of hippies, free spirits and an occasional diet pill, you could fake a natural size 7 and moments of great inspiration were easy. If you hadn't eaten in 3 days and were a little goofy, a creative surge could happen. Now we refer to it as delusion and irresponsibility.

I think we say if you remember the 60's, you weren't there.

Either way, I had a few of those moments back then and as I was doing another one of my great sorting projects, I found poetry written by me. It was so profound that I can't understand it.

I actually was able to remember the exact day I wrote it. Tedious and much too long, double digit pages, handwritten, I sat by the window in a 10th floor apartment in New York City on a fairly pleasant afternoon. I lived in that apartment on the upper east side of Manhattan with 2 roommates and my whole NYC future was looking pretty good.

As I'm sure everyone knows by now, I am not a professional writer. I have ideas about things and get motivated to express myself as each new chapter unfolds in my life. They're interesting to me and a few friends but I think the most fun is when I discover things I've written 20+ years ago.

I can sometimes picture where I was and other times I have absolutely no idea who wrote it or why. It's strange how time alters your memories and perspective even when it's a personal expression captured on paper.

Decade by decade I wrote in different styles.

When my parents passed, I found boxes of memorabilia that now, some 20 years later, I am finally sorting. Among the collections, I discovered letters to my parents and godmother sent from my boarding school in Switzerland. (*And no, I was not a trust fund baby!*)

Apparently I wanted comic books and American candy bars. Not much has changed on the candy bar front but the comic book thing didn't last very long. That was 1959 and for the life of me I will never know why I wanted candy bars when I was sitting in Swiss chocolate country!

My sister found some old letters from the 60's and even has the only photo of me ever taken in a 2-piece bathing suit. It was yellow with big orange polka dots but since I wasn't "itsy bitsy," neither was the bathing suit. It's amazing how I thought I was fat at the time and the truth is I looked pretty good!

The one collection of writings I did find and will treasure forever brought back memories of my parents and how I would write to them as life events were happening. Long distance calls were expensive back then. The letters, the handwriting and the choice of paper are so telling when I look at them now.

Reading all those little gems is a great way to spend an evening.

Roadside art

You can't help noticing things lying on the road when you're driving. So whether you have to steer around them, look away or note the unusual, the mind starts to wander and question how it got there.

Everyone knows red rags come from trucks. They are everywhere! That's a given. If you should see a blue rag, make note.

One shoe is probably not good.

Landscape trucks always drop plants and bags of cuttings usually right in the middle of the road. Sometimes a car hits one and the guy behind gets showered in pine or mesquite that sticks to the car. I've seen a few of those. That stuff is sticky!

Couch pillows are very popular roadside art. For some reason when people move furniture, they put it in the back of a pick-up truck too small to handle the job. Then they must run out of bungee cords and lose at least one or two cushions along the way.

If you're driving to California, the 15 has a variety of droppings every few miles. I've even seen a barbecue, a toilet (in case the public ones are closed I suppose) and the mandatory tires. Watching out for stuff helps pass the time. I've already memorized all the hills, valleys and mountain shapes.

Then there are the things you see that you wouldn't mind taking home. I saw a really awesome ladder in the center lane of the freeway. How about a discarded rocking chair that just needs painting?

Next we move to the leftover campaign signs attached to fences months after the elections. I guess they want to be ready for the next round. The law says they have to be removed but no one actually does it until they seem to get defaced or they fall down on their own. Then the trash guys pick them up.

And let's not forget my profession either. We Realtors are always putting stakes in the ground with our phone numbers and signs. Now we even have flags! We're a tough bunch and have been on front lawns forever. They can't keep us down.

How about orange cones? As soon as you see one, the immediate reaction is "Oh crap, traffic will slow down" and you're in a bad mood. Then you drive 200 feet and they stop! You went through all that stress for nothing.

Sometimes you're alerted by the sound of tire screeches, all to the amusement of landscapers who are already in another subdivision laughing.

Perhaps it's art so someone will paint some garbage on the road, sell it and make a million. After all, who expected Andy Warhol to be famous for a soup can?

Autospeak

The older I get, the more I try to pay attention to what I hear and what I say. I've said things forever and sometimes I want a re-do.

An unusual event starts with "You wouldn't believe it if I told you" and my thought is, why bother? You won't believe it anyway. And the moment is gone.

How about "You have no idea...." while explaining a situation? So if the person has no idea, do you have to educate them first? Otherwise they won't understand the story.

An all-time favorite is "There is nothing worse than...." describes something awful. But is it really that awful? I realize there are millions of things worse but we like the drama.

"At the end of the day" seems to be a summary statement. The first time I heard that, it sounded very original. It isn't.

I even see these things show up on my phone in autocorrect mode. Who made that decision? It certainly wasn't me. And yes, you can turn off the option but that would defeat my whole story.

Let's talk about autocorrect. Whether you use an android or an iPhone, someone out there has decided you need help sending messages. This can be very dangerous as I just found out.

I invited an important client and his family to lunch at McCormick & Schmicks a few weeks back and when I sent him the text, it autocorrected to McCormick & Schmucks. Thank goodness I caught it. That would have not gone over very well at all!

"It's a piece of cake!" Huh? If the meaning is that something is easy, just say so. Apparently, according to a dictionary of idioms, the expression originated in the Royal Air Force in the late 1930's for an easy mission. The precise reference is a mystery just as the simile easy as pie.

At our age, saying things like "You're gonna die laughing" or describing something wonderful as "to die for" has a whole different meaning. Every time I hear myself saying it, I wish I could do a re-take.

Trust me.

Forget Eli. Who was Laura Nyro??

For years I have been having the same argument that the song "Eli's Coming" was sung by the 5th Dimension first and all we hear on throwback radio is the Three Dog Night version. Well, it turns out I was wrong and so were my friends.

I got mixed up because it was actually written and released by its author, Laura Nyro a couple of years before the Three Dog Night recording.

This came up again as I was still perplexed by the meaning of the whole song in the first place. I found it on You Tube only to be reminded what a great artist she really was. Now my memories of listening to her haunting versions of songs she wrote I got teary eyed.

She never revealed the meaning of the song although some speculated on its connection to her Jewish heritage or alternatively a lost or harmful love. Opinions are all over the place so we'll never know because she died of ovarian cancer at the young age of 49 in 1997.

I also know why I was confused about the 5th Dimension. Laura wrote "Wedding Bell Blues," "Sweet Blindness" and "Stoned Soul Picnic" putting them on the music map.

Barbra Streisand sang "Stoney End" and Blood, Sweat & Tears did "And When I Die," both Nyro songs. When "Eli's Coming" was recorded later by Three Dog Night, it took off and her own performance was overshadowed.

The style and passion in her voice is perfection listening to her sing "Walk On By" or "Will You Love Me Tomorrow" even though she didn't write them. We are completely swept away in her sea of emotion.

To really understand late 60's, going to those original artists versions brings me to a very comforting place. I felt included in the music and my voice was heard through them. The true artists of that time knew how to tell a story without beating up our brain cells in the process.

Thank you Laura Nyro. I had forgotten for a while but now I'm back.

There's a note for that

If they stopped making post-it notes, my life would come to a screeching halt. I make sure there are little pads everywhere or my life will be utter chaos.

I think of things, write them immediately and move on. Kitchen, bathroom, in front of the TV, desk, etc. all have stickies to tell me what to do.

TV throws ideas at you but the next day you can't recall what movie you wanted to see or the 800 number for that non-stick wonder pan. Have no fear, there's a note for that!

There are even goofy songs about post-it notes on You-Tube. Who knew?

I was once a very accomplished multi-tasker and could keep track of all my business and personal obligations. Birthdays, anniversaries and dates flashed in my head whenever needed. Now there are small little tugs telling me something is due but I can't recall it clearly so I figure that will just resolve itself later.

Some people don't know the value of a post-it note. They use their phones for all reminders. Since I'm not too skilled at my phone, I still need the note. It's reliable and not subject to power outages, battery failures or technological complications.

And what if the phone autocorrects your note and you do the wrong thing?

I've advanced from refrigerator notes to stickies. Unfortunately the fridge has too many magnets of things that are too cute to take down. There's no room for more.

I can stick a note to the cart in the grocery store right over the face of the guy staring at me from the child seat. And stick it on my old desk phone reminding me to call someone. And on the pile of bills to be paid when I think of it.

They invent flying cars, home smart systems and all sorts of things these days. But for us humans, simplicity and low stress works best. If I have my little yellow note, I will accomplish all my tasks, add checkmarks, throw the note away and relax.

Make note of that!

Failure isn't all it's cracked up to be

Over our lifetimes, we are bound to have a few projects that fail, relationships that fall apart and countless other events that might have worked out a bit more favorably if we had made different choices.

I can definitely catalog my share however I will not write of some great revelation or story of victory over adversity. There are far too many of those and personally I think many are therapy for the authors rather than solutions for the rest of us.

So, you ask, what is this about? Simply put, the failures in my life were deliberate choices. I never set out to fail, but rather to experience something new that ultimately became a colossal disaster.

And this leads me to the definition of truth, a word that gets argued endlessly. It's a matter of what my truth is versus yours and what decisions are made because of it.

When I first met my husband, an attorney who certainly knows what the word "truth" means, we had a very vibrant discussion on real truth, my truth and his truth. (*The more you type and say the word, the more it looks funny too.*)

Picture a group of 4-legged animals on a hillside and someone tells you they are horses. Then you look and one of them looks like a cow. Maybe it's how the light hits it but you see a cow. In your mind it's a cow and so you go get a pail, fully expecting to walk up the hill and milk that cow.

Whether or not it's a cow or a horse, the cow thing is your truth and you made the decision to milk it based on what you truly believed it was. If 25 people told you it was a horse, and you still thought it was a cow, it's a cow!

Hopefully when you get up the hill, you're not stupid enough to milk the horse but that's another column.

Based on what I believed a situation to be, I made decisions. I can honestly say I never failed at anything, but the project may have. My truth lead me down some very interesting trails to be sure. Each time it took a 180, I found a new cow.

My mother armed me well for life. When I needed a little behavior adjustment, she would say "Now what?" It was about the next choice, not laboring over the past.

Now that we're in these golden years, whatever that means, we see lots of cows. Baby boomer life re-imagined is all the rage. I see lots of cows on the hillside which could be due to vision problems or simply an ongoing desire to keep exploring.

We measure success by achieving a goal much like winning a prize. What if the real goal is how much we experience by not winning the prize and zig-zagging all over the place?

Reading self-help books, going to therapy, going back to school and all the clubs, museums and events are there for the taking. Failure is not part of my future and I will always see cows when others see horses on the hillside.

Household mysteries

Everyone in the world (well almost) knows about the sock fairy. If you do laundry and wear socks, sooner or later the sock fairy shows up and there you are with odd socks. You can tie them together but in the end, there's no getting around it. I've accepted that.

I'm still baffled by other laundry mysteries like why all the pockets turn inside out when you wash them. I don't do it. It just happens.

And why do my paper towels tear up after use but put them in the wash accidentally and they come out like new. Kleenex has about a 50/50 success rate.

Moving on to the kitchen, every Thanksgiving we buy a turkey baster. Last year I was sure I had at least 5 or 6 of them so I didn't bother getting a new one. As usual, there was not a one to be found in the house. I had plenty of string to sew up the turkey but alas, no baster. It probably went the way of the socks.

How about spatulas? The only one I still have is about 40 to 50 years old with a green handle and it belonged to my parents. But I recall buying a cute set of silicone ones, getting some from casino promotions and seeing several in the drawer. Where did all of them go? And most curiously, is my mother's spatula holding some secret power that makes it appear every time I need it? Maybe it scares off all the younger spatulas.

The most annoying of all kitchen tales has got to be lids and containers. Show me one person on the planet who can tell me they have never had mismatching lids and containers. I even bought a set where there are only 3 sizes and all the lids are interchangeable. I think they shrunk because now they don't all fit.

Storage space holds the quite a challenge too. How is it that when you organize your entire home, clear out older things and have leftover shelf space, it magically fills up while you sleep! No one went shopping or received gifts but somehow those clean cabinets are spilling over with crap.

And last but not least is the collection of mugs coming out of the dishwasher. Buy one more mug as a souvenir of places visited and the whole balance of the kitchen dish cabinet is thrown off. I spend too much time making all the handles line up for that one extra little guy that reminds me of a great vacation.

As trivial as this all is, the answers still escape me. I'm headed to the dollar store to buy spatulas.

The digital dilemma

That moment when you realize that in spite of all you've done to get the best deal or trim the extras, everything is getting more and more expensive and your fixed income is not keeping up.

I have never been one to divide a lunch check down to the nickel or pitch in for a gift and ask for a receipt. If you are sharing, just do it. If it varies $5 or $10, who cares?

Now as prices go up and benefits go down, we live in an age where every new technological product has become a "must have" whether you like it or not. Liking it is not my issue. I can't always afford it and then I'm out of the loop.

We watch the Emmys and all the awards go to cable company extras and suddenly my TV costs $100, my internet costs $60 and a land line costs $39. Add the tax and an occasional movie add-on, and we're well over $200 a month. Watching a movie is another $7. How insane!

If you want an antenna for free TV, good luck. The company tells you because of the mountains, you'll only get 2 networks and some weird channels.

Let's take the phone lines. If you want to have a land line in case there's some kind of problem with your digital services, it won't work anyway because it's hard wired to your digital service. So much for that back-up idea.

If your cell phone needs help to get signal in some areas, the next step is begging your cell provider for a booster. It helps a bit, however I find it's only good in a 10 square foot area of my house. Since several communities don't permit cell towers, we're out of luck for now.

Then come the internet charges. A personal favorite of mine for sure. I have been upgraded many times for free they say. Now I'm upgraded to the newest version and it is a miserable experience.

I can't dump my trash emails, it won't respond when I want to fix spam settings and countless other annoying things are happening. And, my computer is slower but my speed with the company is considered higher. Huh?

I asked for the old version but they wouldn't give it to me. Then they said my 20 year discount isn't really available now that I have the latest version. Who asked for it anyway!?!?

If I switch my TV to another company who uses my same email provider, I can't have my same email address. Good one guys.

So the moment is here and decisions are pending. Grab the foil and rabbit ears!

Insect spray in the bread aisle!

There are times when you look at something and you know it's just not right. So when I went grocery shopping the other day, they were completely re-arranging all the aisles, putting shelves up front so you can't even see the store and generally making a mess.

Some marketing genius at corporate is at it again making deciding how I want to shop. Again folks, grocery shopping is not a resort destination activity!

If they wanted me to notice some new items, wouldn't it make sense to put it in an area I already frequent so it would stand out?

Nope. These scholars completely upset the order of things that I just figured out from the last time they did it.

This is right up there with driving 10 miles to save 10 cents a gallon on gas, or collecting hundreds of Monopoly pieces, sticking them on a piece of paper and hoping for $5.00.

And then I saw it. In the new bread aisle was a display on the shelf for insect spray. Seriously? I'm not too sure about the mind trigger on that.

Who thinks about insect spray when they're buying bread and bagels? If you do think about it, you must need an exterminator anyway, not to mention that stuff getting close to your food.

And speaking of the bread aisle, why did they take it away from the bakery section? So for a year or so, I've been running back and forth from one end of the store to the other to find what kind of breakfast pastry we want. There was a time when they were all together but alas, the fun is over.

The brilliance behind all these marketing plans has nothing to do with actual people. There's an algorithm somewhere using artificial intelligence to send us into a state of confusion when doing something we have to do to survive.

All of these changes are called "convenient" by the marketers. Is it convenient to chase around like a lunatic when you're finishing a work day and need to grab 3 things? Is it convenient to go through a web based app to get grocery discounts so they can monitor your habits and sell them to others?

Is it OK to be made to feel guilty when you put in your debit card and they ask for donations? You actually get a multiple choice of what to donate. How rude!

One smart thing they've done is add a donation box at the register to drop in change. I like that and do it all the time. Same thing with McDonald's at the drive-thru. Very easy and not offensive.

I donate but, for heaven sakes, leave me alone!

We have reached the end of our patience with donation robo-calls, checkout counters asking for donations, TV ads, and even ATM machines!

It seems the world is getting in on an old play well documented in my family history. GUILT! If I say no in front of the supermarket cashier, I look like a mean old lady.

Get away to a casino and put a cash ticket into the ATM and it asks if you want to donate a percentage of that ticket. At least you have a choice of a few charities and after all, these may be gambling winnings and you'll go to a fiery place if you don't share your good luck. More guilt!

The calls can be very interesting too. There's this man from a police fund who sounds completely irritated when you say no and I have fear that if I call 911 from the same number, no one will come. What to do? Guilt now mixed with fear.

Another call tells me about children, another about veterans and the list goes on. And the calls never stop so we started blocking numbers. That did absolutely nothing because they never call from the same number more than once.

My husband is a veteran, I love kids and I am passionate about animals. We go through all the mailers every few months and take everything into consideration and support multiple causes to the best of our ability.

We even donated for a cow or goat to enable a 3rd world country family to have milk. They didn't assault me in the grocery store to get my attention. I read about it and liked what I read. I've never seen a program like that in the U.S.

The same is true for several veterans' organizations. Read about it and make your decision based on the things you care about, not guilt.

If anything, these tactics may work on some but I find them incredibly offensive so just because of that, I will probably choose something else.

I'm kind of OK on displays of food bags. At least it's a silent choice and grabbing one at the checkout is up to me.

If I get too many mailers with "gifts," that tells me they're possibly spending an awful lot of my donation money on marketing and not helping. I suppose I should thank them for the thousands of address labels we've received.

In the end, we do our part and are very grateful for the privileged life we lead. But for heaven's sake, leave me alone!

Hacking, fraud & security can take over your life!

If you've ever had an account, email or credit card hacked, you already know what an absolute nightmare it can be to straighten things out. But we experienced something even more frustrating. One credit card fraud department actually reported on the wrong transactions!

It is amazing to me how a fraud alert turned into endless phone calls lasting over 3 hours each. It really happened and I watched the timer on my phone register 3 hours and 17 minutes. That was just the 1st day.

This sets off a series of events that are impossible to correct once the mistake is made. Everyone is connected to credit bureaus and your reports are instantly filled with bad information so other vendors get spooked and change the terms of other accounts.

If you try to go back to report the original problem to correct your record, the computerized response says no because the report came from another computer that told the first computer.

There are no humans involved in any of this. But rest assured computers have friends! Remember the old commercial "They told 2 friends, and they told 2 friends....?"

It took about 8 to 10 months for things to smooth out and then I looked at all the different accounts using fraudulent information to rate me.

Fortunately I really didn't care much since no matter how perfect we are on paper, something is bound to screw it up. I learned the smallest things can send you into chaos. We are automated into oblivion!

Now we come to the passwords. What an adventure that is! I keep a list of them in a secret place because I can't even trust these apps to guard my information. If my dogs ever get that piece of paper, I'm completely out of business.

Another personal favorite (I always have personal favorites) is the double and triple levels of verification when they text you another 6 to 10 digit code to pay a bill.

In our home, I do the bills and naturally on my husband's

accounts they list his phone number. So the rush is on to request the code and then run all over the house to find his phone, look at it and get back to the computer before it expires and we have to call all over again.

That process always gets interrupted because he wants to know why I'm snooping through his phone. Next step is to change the phone number on his accounts to mine and avoid the question.

With all the levels of so-called security, I have never experienced so much fraud and confusion over just paying life's expenses! Once in a while a check was lost but you called the bank and wrote another one. No one "washed" my checks or re-routed my credit cards to Miami.

There was one experience that made me smile recently when I discovered we were getting automatically charged for something not once, but twice. The credit card company called the vendor for a 3-way call. They listened and got so annoyed because the vendor could not even see the charges so he hung up on them and credited the whole thing, blocking them from our account.

A giant step for the consumer!

Sliced bread has nothing on this!

An expression we all grew up with is "I haven't seen anything like this since sliced bread!" I'm still not sure why that was such an accomplishment but I imagine it was significant at the time.

But in my opinion 2 things completely blow sliced bread out of the water! How about elastic and zippers?

As body parts relocate and buttons are harder to use when you're arthritic, elastic and zippers make life better, adjusting to changes and always reliable.

Zippers keep everything in order. There are plastic bags with zippers, pants, mattress covers, tents and millions of things that close neatly and tightly as needed.

And elastic! The best of the best! It lets you squeeze into things when your body shouldn't be wearing it. Spandex fabric, stretchy waists and all pull-on clothes rely on it so we can say we wear a size smaller than we really do.

So who do we have to thank for all that?

It was Thomas Hancock, an Englishman who founded the British rubber industry in the early 1800's. He invented the masticator, a machine that shredded rubber scraps and allows rubber to be recycled after being formed into blocks or rolled sheets. The process of creating elastic fabrics required a lot of trial & error until he used heat & pressure to unite the pieces for some purposes.

And the zipper came from an 1851 patent for an "Automatic Continuous Clothing Closure" invented by Elias Howe. His invention acted as more of a drawstring and in 1891, Whitcomb Judson marketed a "Clasp Locker" that served as more of a hook-and-eye shoe fastener. Eventually development lead by Gideon Sundback, a Swedish-American engineer gave us the "Separable Fastener" patented in 1917.

In the 1920's zippers showed up on leather jackets and in the 1930's sales campaigns for children's clothing featured zippers. By 1937, zippers for men's trousers were all the rage.

The stories are far more detailed than I've written here but suffice it to say, these guys made sliced bread look blah!

Next episode is staples.

Pantyhose, watermelons & tire irons

We're sitting at dinner with friends and the subject of home gardens comes up. We live in the blasted desert and our friend is growing a supermarket full of veggies and fruit!

Apparently there are a zillion tricks to everything so I found a few more here and there.

Yes our friend is right about the pantyhose and watermelons. Believe it or not, by putting the watermelon in pantyhose it keeps it free of bugs. People also keep them suspended from the ground that way too. (I looked it up to be sure.) So the next time you see "hanging" watermelons, look a little closer. They might be dressed up and wearing pantyhose.

As for the tire irons, we learned this years ago that burying one in the ground next to a tree emits something to make the tree grow bigger and stronger. We did that and the tree went nuts.

We had one problem though. The second time we also used it to keep the tree steady so the tip was showing on the ground and the HOA came and ticketed us. Whoever was marching around the neighborhood had to really work at finding it buried in the lawn so we just pushed it in further and ignored them. Some people just don't have anything important to do so they creep around looking for things. I never saw that rule in the guidelines.

Next are bunny issues. You can spend weeks looking up desert friendly flowers that rabbits don't eat or building chicken wire fences, tall garden stands or hanging baskets. I found all sorts of sites listing rabbit resistant plants but they don't all agree.

I picked some gazanias and found out I was wrong however, if you put rosemary sprigs around, they don't get eaten! Problem is the sprigs dry up so every week you can cut fresh ones if you're that committed.

I think we're down to lantana now. I searched for color varieties and have learned to like them. I don't have any patience so the veggie thing is out.

So what can go wrong?

2020 is the year that we wish would just end already. As always when a new year begins, we say it's going to be better but this one failed miserably.

Personally I have suffered some overwhelming losses due to this pandemic and my vision of life going forward has been altered permanently. But I actually found a little humor in my daily challenges just trying to stay "normal."

I have realized that if no one is home and I push the wrong button on the TV remote, I will never watch television again. Since my vision has changed a bit, I can't tell the guide button from the exit button and the list goes on. A call to the cable company usually results in a charge to come and re-program everything.

Moving to the garage, I noticed water on the floor in strange places. The first place to look is the water heater. Been there, done that. Nope, that's not it. So it rained that day. You remember that one day, right? When the garage door opened, it dripped a bit. So maybe that was it and I don't have a disaster. Nope, wrong again.

After three days of watching water move around like a river with no destination, I happened to peek into my water softener and sure enough it was filled with water where the salt goes. Lo and behold, my home warranty doesn't cover that. How nice for me. More money spent.

One day I came home to that horrible noise of the smoke detector blasting every 5 seconds. I put the dogs as far away from it as I could, found batteries and made the precarious climb up the ladder to fix the problem. It wasn't the batteries. Apparently our smoke detectors burn themselves out after a while and it's got to go.

The timer on my lights has not kept up with the seasons and I tried to adjust it but alas, all I did was mess it up even more.

That was my week. How was yours?

Bending, sitting & opening straws

I am noticing those subtle changes that happen as you grow into seniorhood. Some of us do it gracefully, some hardly show it at all and others of us get caught up in the little annoying things. I'm part of the last group.

Straws with plastic wrapping drive me nuts. If you slam it down on the table to break the seal on the wrapper, the straw bends and it's still closed. If you try to tear it, it's a 5-minute process but eventually it will split open.

Shrink-wrapped cucumbers are another packaging problem because you have to use a knife and then peel it away. What if you want to keep half the cucumber? Give it a chop and hope for the best.

Pull-top cans have always been an issue. I once sliced my hand open and now I am terrified of them. I can insert the handle part of a utensil and then wrap the top in a towel before pulling. That's a project all for a tuna sandwich but I like tuna. Now they have some gadgets to help but I can't find the ad. It's somewhere in the cloud.

What if your doctor says "no seeds" for your dietary guidelines? Try explaining that in a drive-thru burger place.

And fork-split English muffins? Someone told me to cut it but then the nooks and crannies are gone. I must be clumsy because they all come out thin on one side and fat side gets stuck in the toaster.

And last is the problem when something falls on the floor. Lord help me if it rolls under the bed! The first challenge is getting there before the dog. Then when I have to get on the floor, it requires strategic planning to get back up again.

Bending and sitting are still relatively intact for now. Still dealing with smoke alarm battery changes, yard work, garage clutter and air filters on my own. What used to be no big deal now calls for supervision or caution.

Wasn't ready for this!

Don't get caught!

So you think we have some crazy laws here in Nevada? Think again. The wild state of Texas has outdone itself and these laws are still on the books:

- Criminals who intend on committing crimes must give their victims oral or written notice 24 hours in advance and include the nature of the crime.
- It is illegal to dust a public building with a feather duster.
- It is illegal to shoot a buffalo from the second story of a hotel.
- You must have a $5.00 permit to walk around barefoot.
- Throw out those Encyclopedias! The Encyclopedia Britannica is banned in Texas because it contains a formula for making beer.
- You cannot buy beer on Sunday in Houston after midnight but you can buy it on Monday.
- When two trains meet each other at a railroad crossing, they both must stop and neither shall proceed until the other has gone.
- It is legal for a chicken to have sex with you but it's illegal to reciprocate.
- It is illegal to shoot an Indian from a streetcar.
- In Texarkana, owners of horse may not ride them at night without taillights.
- It is illegal to drive without windshield wipers. You don't need a windshield but you must have the wipers.

But, getting back to Nevada, here's a couple I'll bet you never knew:

- It is illegal to drive a camel on the highway.

You don't see many of those.

- As of 2010, you can not have hula hoops more than 4 feet in diameter on Fremont Street.

No contests, folks!

And to top it all off, this takes the cake:

- It is illegal in Liverpool UK for a woman to be topless except as a clerk in a tropical fish store.

I have no idea what to say for a change.

There are dozens of insane laws on the books of all states and if you want to have a fun read, google crazy laws and laugh yourself silly.

Paraproskodian

I just learned a new word and although it is a mouthful to repeat, the meaning is a sentence with an unexpected ending. In Greek it is "against expectations" and humorists use them all the time.

When Groucho Marx exclaimed "I've had a perfectly wonderful evening, but this wasn't it" it was a paraprosdokian.

And Zsa Zsa Gabor said "He taught me housekeeping; when I divorce, I keep the house."

Some of the most serious people have said the most unexpected things:

- Thomas Jefferson once said 'We should never judge a president by his age, only by his works.' And ever since he told me that, I stopped worrying. — *Ronald Reagan*
- We can always count on the Americans to do the right thing, after they have exhausted all other possibilities. — *Winston Churchill*
- People say I'm indecisive, but I don't know about that. —*George H. W. Bush*
- Three may keep a secret, if two of them are dead. —*Benjamin Franklin*
- Blessed are the young for they shall inherit the national debt. —*Herbert Hoover*
- I have the heart of a small boy — in a glass jar on my desk. —*Stephen King*

A little creepy but totally unexpected, nonetheless.

Just for fun, here are a few more from the internet not credited to anyone in particular:

- To steal ideas from one person is plagiarism. To steal from many is research.

- Knowledge is knowing a tomato is a fruit. Wisdom is not putting it in a fruit salad.

- In filling out an application where it says "In case of emergency, notify," answer "a doctor."

- Since light travels faster that sound, some people appear bright until you hear them speak.

- Women will never be equal to men until they can walk down the street with a bald head and a beer gut and still think they are sexy.

- You're never too old to learn something stupid.

And although some may seem insulting, they are said in fun only. But this last one got my attention:

- Going to church doesn't make you a Christian any more than standing in a garage makes you a car.

On the Road

Vegas normal

This is probably the most unusual town in the whole country where our "normal" would defy all logic anywhere else. Not a surprise to anyone but I am always amused by expectations when I travel outside the state.

Take a grocery store for example. Most of them are the same whether you're here, California, Arizona or even Jersey. But when it's time to check out, you "play a 20" and recover your grocery money or even more. Where else can you go into a store and come out with money AND groceries?

Let's talk gifts from hotels. You frequent a hotel/casino and get a slot card. Put that card in once in a while and gift notices start flooding your mailbox. Go on Tuesday and you pick up a glassware set. Go on Thursday and it's bed linen day.

Getting ready for vacation, I actually scheduled my day around what I might need. I have two beach umbrellas, one beach chair (I missed a day) and a cooler, picnic basket and duffel on wheels. Our beach week was handled.

And booze! We don't drink but I have the most exotic collection of liquor ever. Flavored vodka, wine in many shades of grape, scotch, bourbon, brandy, Turkey this and Jack that. Some are in slightly smaller sizes but it's quite impressive when I have this assortment to offer friends.

Planning for gifts is easier too. Collect dishes, colorful cookware and home accessories over the year and you're done. My daughter caught on and now she peeks in the cabinet to see what duplicates we may have. It lightens the load for me and I make room for the next batch.

Many cities call themselves 24-hour towns but only in Nevada do they really mean it. People who would not step out alone after dark now drive home at 2AM and think nothing of it. This is Vegas and everyone's up.

Our city offers diversity on so many levels and yet, we're sometimes perceived as a shallow minded population in the desert with no purpose. Many don't realize the genius it takes to build a place like this. The creativity and expertise to draw an international audience is unmatched anywhere in the world. We set the bar very high to make the city wheels turn.

Yes, the highest income is earned in gaming and not everyone participates. If you do, you get stuff and you win back your grocery money once in a while. You eat for free but in reality, that cup of coffee probably cost $100.

While everyone is coming here for vacation, I'm taking my toys and going elsewhere. It feels different in the grocery store and the streets go dark at 9PM. Who does that?

I no longer mind explaining we don't live in the basements of casinos. If someone wants to imagine Vegas life, I'm perfectly happy letting them do it. After all, it only adds to the mystique of living here.

On vacation I have to train myself to ask where to go for dinner instead of asking how many points I have. Yup, this is Vegas normal.

Senior travel check list

When I first wrote about the dating checklist, I didn't imagine that as you become more and more familiar with each other, all sorts of other checklists come up.

After passing all the dating tests, we've started traveling. I have been elevated to social director and since he's retired and I'm not, he leaves the planning to me. New checklists everywhere!

First of all, neither one of us can remember things for more than 10 minutes on a good day so preparing for travel begins 2 weeks in advance.

It starts with traumatizing the dogs as suitcases get laid out. Anything I put in has a risk of being taken out and hidden. It's a treasure hunt for them. I think I will win but inevitably discover their mischief when I'm already gone.

When packing, the usual climate questions are pretty easy but underwear definitely requires thought. What if we're somewhere with no civilized bathroom? These days no one gets much warning when it's that time and adult diapers are a consideration. How many? One for each day or is that overkill?

And medications are a biggie. We went overseas last month and my entire carry-on was filled with prescriptions. The normal daily ones are in pretty compact weekly plastic boxes. But what about a sinus infection or a cut or ankle twist? Got the ace & regular bandages, every kind of antibiotic, upset stomach, constipation and the opposite problem, allergy sprays, cough meds, ointments for itches or scrapes, etc. etc. You develop this fear of being without so dragging everything along seems appropriate.

The final meds for us require they be kept cold. There's the carry-on lunch bag with an old-fashioned screw-top ice bag and our shots. That gets filled at least once a day, every day. And you have to explain to TSA that it's OK so they put it in a machine to check if it's explosive.

Shoe choices are a breeze. For those of us that can only wear flats these days, I have flip-flops and Sketchers. Other than those I don't care anymore. Kind of nice to have that easy a decision.

Now we come to the canes, walkers, braces and dentures.

Which cane? The pretty one from Amazon or the ugly one from Walgreens for strokes? (*The pretty one won.*) The walker or scooter is only a last resort for now.

For those of us with declining knees, just try and find a pretty knee brace. Not happening so the ugly Velcro thing will have to do. And partial dentures that I dislike intensely are in a little box in my purse. I hate them but when it's picture time, out they come!

I am a tech-stupid senior but nevertheless I have a laptop, cell phone & smart watch. I take them in the hope I won't have to use them. Makes sense to me anyway.

So we travel and hobble around. We have become "those" people on the tourist buses taking 5 minutes just to get off the thing. Hate us all you want but we're having a great time!

I am a tourist

We live in an amazing city and we forget what it's like to be on the other side of a tourism economy. So when we get the chance to visit elsewhere, it's hard not to notice what it's like to be THE tourist for a change.

When we go to gift shops in other lands, the first order of business is to buy something cute and adorable for my granddaughter that she will play with for about 10 minutes. So what if it costs $50.00. That's not the point!

The next part is when we get creative and find another gift that will make noise. We just found junior bagpipes in Scotland. Naturally I got the matching jacket to go with it. Yes, I'm sure my daughter will hate me. In Ireland I found a small Guernsey cow and a pretty t-shirt and another sheep in Scotland to go with everything else. In England there was a Paddington bear.

When we were at the beach earlier in the summer it was a mermaid and a music box.

As for us, our grown-up gifts are whiskey fudge, books of all the places we go and tiny highland cows and sheep for the bookshelf. I have absolutely no place for anything else. Oh yes, also a huge bill from the cruise ship that I will treasure always.

People are nice when you visit other countries. You have big eyes and you're looking to soak up the surroundings so any memento offered is greatly appreciated. As soon as you mention a grandchild, the suggestions start flowing. Each one is noisier than the last and it empowers grandparents.

Say you hail from Las Vegas and they smile knowingly. Not sure why.

The tours are kind of fun too. Guides are proud of their country but you can't see anything from a bus. They need to put bubble tops on them so you don't take a picture of the head in the seat in front of you.

And that's why I buy the books and my coffee table will collapse soon.

Blowin' in the wind

What wind? Do we have wind? Just another day in Las Vegas sitting behind glass patio doors watching our outdoor furniture go flying by.

Other days I find myself hugging 73 pounds of dog because she hears thunder 25 miles away with the wind. Her majesty has broken the record for holding it so she doesn't have to brave the elements.

The wind seems to be at its best the night before trash pick-up. The bins flip open and all the coyotes know what night it is. That makes for double fun the next morning.

My deliveries of small items always seem to arrive on windy days too. The large cartons of dog food wait until the rain hits but little stuff bounces along the rocks until I run around and catch it.

Wind in southern Nevada has a character all its own. One side of the Las Vegas valley can be calm and the other has dancing dust devils all over the place.

Rain is like that too. Ominous clouds hang over one neighborhood surrounded by blue sky everywhere else.

When summer comes, we get all excited about wind because it will cool us off from the blazing heat. Nope. Not going to happen.

We have what we affectionately call "the blow dryer effect" in the summer. A blast of warm air engulfs you, messes up that cute summer hairdo and your body gets all mixed up. You've just left an overly air-conditioned building, walked out into the heat and now get into your car which is baking in the sun. You turn on your car air conditioner and it blasts you again with hot air until you've traveled a few miles.

In the fall we wait patiently for it to cool down a bit. The breezes seem a little more manageable and the temperature drops somewhere between October and November.

This year however, nothing was normal and it seemed like the winds blew almost every day. But I'm grateful we're not in the Midwest dealing with tornadoes so a little wind is OK.

Home is where the good toilet paper is

I've been really fortunate to travel several times this year. Ships, hotels, car rides, lots of new restaurants, sight-seeing, and all sorts of new adventures. And then I come home exhausted and happy.

What really makes me happy is having an actual full-size bathroom with the toilet paper of my choice. Cruise ships and public places never have decent toilet paper. You wind up pulling out long reams of the stuff just to fold it up so you can't see through it. I agree it must adhere to regulations for recycling on a ship but it's nice to get home to the good stuff. And seat covers? Where are they?

So the food starts out really wonderful coupled with good service. Then on about the 3rd day it all begins to taste the same. Steak tastes like chicken, fish has the same sauce as the other chicken and so on. Soups and sorbet are really good. After a while you begin to find ways to customize your meals and everyone makes fun of you for being so fussy. (Actually that's me)

Cruise ships and hotels make your bed up every day. I hate making beds or doing dishes so those are a win-win for me.

Coffee in my cabin is a luxury.

Packing is OK because you're GOING somewhere. The problems start with me when I come back and have to unpack. That's right up there with the dishes and laundry so I put it off for a day or so. About a week goes by and I just keep staring at it hoping things will jump out on their own and put themselves away. They don't so I drudgingly start sorting it out.

The little things can make you crazy like when you forget a hair clip or don't pack enough underwear so you're trotting off to the laundry room on the ship. But when you get home, you're happy and sad at the same time doing the laundry.

And let's not forget the toilet paper! It's good to be home.

www.ingramcontent.com/pod-product-compliance
Lightning Source LLC
LaVergne TN
LVHW050637100826
845148LV00011B/1893

* 9 7 9 8 2 1 8 4 1 6 7 1 3 *

"Charlie Drew's deep knowledge and love of the Psalms are on full display in this invaluable volume. In addition to his learning, there is deep passion and love, not only for the Psalms, but for the Savior who sang them. I found myself weeping numerous times as I read—tears of joy, and love for Jesus. I hope you have the same experience."

—KATHY KELLER, co-author of *The Songs of Jesus: A Year of Daily Devotions in the Psalms*

"When Charlie Drew expounds the Scripture, he is always wonderfully Christ-centered—and not in a superficial or repetitious way. He knows the many and varied theological themes running through all the Bible, and he knows how to follow them carefully until they all meet in Jesus Christ. His book on the Psalms is no exception. I recommend it."

—TIM KELLER, Founder, Redeemer Presbyterian Church

"This book about the Psalms will help them sing even more deeply in your heart. It shows you how Psalms give voice to Jesus' own experience. The image of Jesus Christ actually lives, thinks, feels, and speaks. And it is this very image that he wishes to form in us."

—DAVID POWLISON, Executive Director (2014–2019), Christian Counseling and Education Foundation

"In the quietness of your most private place, take a few moments to let Charlie Drew walk you through verses that you've recited in church or breezed through in haste and distraction. You will discover not only the God you barely know, but how deeply he already knows you."

—PETER C. MOORE, Founder, Fellowship of Christians in Universities and Schools

"Charlie Drew helps us recognize that we hear not only the voice of the psalmist who helps us pray but the voice of Jesus himself who said that all the Psalms spoke of him. I recommend *Singing with Emmanuel* to all Christians who want to know the Psalms, and, more importantly, Jesus better."

—TREMPER LONGMAN III, Distinguished Scholar and Professor Emeritus of Biblical Studies, Westmont College

"Through this imaginative and distinctly Christian approach to the Psalms, you will hear Jesus speaking in an intensely personal way about his own life, death, and resurrection. You will come to know Jesus and the gospel more intimately and more deeply. A profoundly edifying experience!"

—DOUGLAS GREEN, Professor of Old Testament, Queensland Theological College, Australia

"For two thousand years the Psalms have been adopted by the Christian Church as our own hymn book. But now Charlie Drew invites us to encounter them in a completely fresh way—by hearing the voice of Jesus speaking to us through them. Charlie leads us to discover new dimensions of understanding and new depths of worship in a book we thought we knew so well."

—JOHN W. HOWE, Bishop, Anglican Church in North America

"Charlie Drew writes with the passion of a dynamic preacher, the insights of a biblical scholar, the language of a fine poet, and the honesty of a close friend. As we are challenged to see the Psalms through the eyes of Jesus, we understand both their purpose and his grace in new ways."

—NEIL LEBHAR, Assisting Bishop, Gulf Atlantic Diocese, Anglican Church in North America

"When I read the Psalms as the prayers, joys, fears, despairs, and delights of Jesus, I'm reminded that Jesus really has walked in my shoes. *Singing with Emmanuel* has shown me Jesus not only as my king who has saved me, but also as my loving brother who has experienced every aspect of humanity in order to empathize with me completely."

—SARAH DREW, Actor

"Charlie Drew's understanding of the Psalms opens a window to see the authentic Jesus. The writing is precise and personal, the interpretations are compelling, and the overall effect is a powerful volume in which the Psalms come alive in new ways."

—FRANK GUERRA, Headmaster Emeritus, Boston Trinity Academy

"I will never read the Psalms the same way again. Forever more, I will have the posture of praying the Psalms alongside my older brother Jesus who alone lived them and prayed them perfectly and beautifully."

—KEVIN NIEMANN, Strategic Partnership Director for Churches, World Relief

"Heart-felt spirituality and thoughtful biblical reading . . . intellectually provocative and winsome . . . the loving work of a pastor who leads the reader through practical helps, prayers, and guidelines to experience the Psalms in ever enriching ways. I recommend it wholeheartedly."

—JIM BLACK, Director of Fellowship of Christian Athletes, Stanford University

"I've long appreciated Charlie Drew's gift for helping readers make the connection between the Bible and the Christian life without reducing it to slogans or formulas. *Singing with Emmanuel* brings to bear the richness of biblical theology and the heart of a pastor. Earlier generations spoke of the need for an 'experimental knowledge of Christ' that is both born of the richness of our communion with God and led by a full understanding of his Word. This book stands in that tradition. Highly recommended."

—TOM CANNON, Former National Coordinator, Reformed University Ministries

"What a tremendous contribution Charlie Drew has made to our experience of the book of Psalms. Thank you for linking Jesus to the Psalms as you have."

—LARRY E. CHRISTENSEN, Director, City Leadership Network

"The world-changing story of Jesus has become the story of his people as a whole—past, present, and future. This has deep implications for the Psalms. Charlie Drew guides us pastorally into the practice of reading the Psalter in the mysterious reality of this union. Highly recommended."

—ALLEN DREW, East Coast Director, Climate Witness Project

"Charlie Drew does not avoid the troublesome passages that I am tempted to skip over—David's outrageous claims of innocence or his vindictive curses of vengeance on his enemies. Listening for Jesus' voice and story in them—and in all the Psalms—has helped me understand and embrace them. It has also deepened my experience of his costly love for humanity and his astonishing willingness to identify with his fallen, fragile followers, whom he calls brothers and sisters."

—MARDI KEYES, Co-founder, L'Abri Fellowship, Southborough, Massachusetts

"Pastor Drew does not want us to read the Psalms and just be encouraged. We are settling for too little! He wants the Psalms to help us understand Jesus' own heart more deeply as we pray these Psalms as his prayers."

—GRACE KIM, MD, Associate Professor of Surgery, University of Michigan